Healing t

CW00417842

The 6-step healing guide to overcoming the legacy of Emotionally Immature, Toxic, and Abusive Parents!

A personal journey:

Understand, heal, be happy, and live fully.

By
Norma Caceres-Pell

Legal Notice:

Disclaimer Notice:

Please note the information contained within this document is for educational and entertainment purposes only. All effort has been expended to present accurate, up-to-date, and reliable, complete information. No warranties of any kind are declared or implied. Readers acknowledge that the author is not engaging in the rendering of legal, financial, medical, or professional advice. The content within this book has been derived from various sources. Please consult a licensed professional before attempting any techniques outlined in this book.

By reading this document, the reader agrees that under no circumstances is the author responsible for any losses, direct or indirect, which are incurred as a result of the use of the information contained within this document, including, but not limited to, — errors, omissions, or inaccuracies.

Table of Contents

Introduction

Whenever I walk the ***Sendero of the Iguazu Falls***, my body vibrates with excitement as if it knows something special will happen, and indeed, it does every time. Standing in front of the immensity of these waters and the staggering beauty of mother nature is like pressing the reset button, like being washed from everything that happened before and being allowed to start again; it is undoubtedly very healing. Mother Nature has a tremendous healing power, the power to put things in perspective and give us the strength to reassess objectively and continue our path. Having this thought present as I worked through healing the scars that the experiences with my parents left in me has been fundamental as it reminded me that we are all unique individuals with our baggage, capable of doing great things as well as making great mistakes but overall lovable with the right to happiness like anybody else on this earth.

Inevitably, our past experiences with those meant to nurture and guide us—our parents— would have left profound imprints on our personas and influenced how we see the world. Parents are beacons of love, support, and wisdom for most people, providing the foundation upon which we build our lives and become happy selves. But what if, instead of a solid foundation, our childhood was marked by emotional immaturity, neglect, or even abuse? What if the people meant to protect us left us with scars that seemed impossible to heal?

Being an adult child of an *"Emotionally immature, Abusive, and Toxic Parent"* is a challenging experience. It could affect all aspects of our lives, starting with our relationships with other people and our psychological and mental health, which could, in turn, affect our physical health. These are the reasons why I believe it is fundamental to analyse, understand, and deal with the traumas we may have due to these experiences, some of which we may not even be aware of.

Gaining perspective on these situations has certainly been life-changing for me. Understanding the lasting impact of the relationship with our emotionally immature and abusive parents is critically important for several reasons:

Self-Healing: Recognising and understanding the impact of emotional abuse is the first step towards healing and recovery. It allows us to acknowledge our pain and begin the process of self-care and self-compassion, which is a challenging but crucial step.

Breaking the Cycle: By recognising unhealthy patterns and taking responsibility, we can make conscious choices to avoid repeating them in our relationships and with our children or loved ones.

Empowerment: recognising the effects of emotional abuse can empower us to make positive changes in our lives. It can give us the insight and motivation to seek therapy or support groups, set boundaries, and make healthier choices.

Validation: I often see survivors of emotional abuse minimise or deny their experiences, making it more difficult for them to avoid the vicious circle, repeat the whole thing, and accept that what they went through was wrong and harmful.

Emotional Regulation: People who have been emotionally abused can often find difficulties in regulating their emotions. Understanding how our upbringing has affected our emotional responses can help us develop healthier coping mechanisms and emotional regulation skills.

Healthy Relationships: Forming and maintaining healthy relationships can be challenging if you carry emotional scars from an abusive upbringing. Understanding the impact that these experiences can have on us can help us work on building more beneficial connections with all the people around us.

Self-Esteem: Emotional abuse can severely impact self-esteem and self-worth; this is something that I have struggled with hugely, and it has taken me many years to overcome. Putting everybody else's needs first and being a people pleaser have taken me to do things for others to my detriment. Understanding these lasting effects can help to rebuild our self-esteem and self-confidence.

Mental Health: Emotional abuse is directly linked to mental health issues such as anxiety, depression, and post-traumatic stress disorder (PTSD). Understanding the impact of our experiences can guide us toward seeking appropriate mental health support and treatment.

Recovery: Recovery from an emotionally abusive upbringing is a journey. Understanding the impact is a crucial step in this journey, as it provides a roadmap for your personal growth and healing.

When searching for a title, someone suggested **"Surviving Childhood Abuse",** which I thought was good. However, the issues with my parents became more challenging as my childhood ended and the abuse worsened. Up until not long ago and for most of my life, I spent loads of time trying to find ways to please my mother and provide for my family, but it always felt like I was in a race I could never win, I could never satisfy my mother and all her demands. She always made me feel guilty and responsible for everything, from the house bills and maintenance to anything my younger siblings needed or wanted. I was programmed to believe anything that went wrong within my family was my responsibility. No matter how much I tried, it would never be enough.

Getting this Book right is essential for me for many reasons, and here are some of them.

1- Many people endure constant pain and suffering because they tolerate mistreatment from their parents or family members simply because they share a family connection.

2- Other people recognise they are being abused but live hoping that these individuals will change and they will, at some point, have a good relationship with them.

3-Others don't know how to deal with their abusive family and the damage that these relationships may be causing them.

We must go through these stages to overcome abuse and regain control of our lives. However, I often see people stuck in a vicious circle, hoping for a change that will never come, and they convince themselves there is no better way.

After all these years, I have realised that these experiences could bring other more significant issues to our physical, psychological, and mental health if left unsolved. For all these reasons, it is fundamental to face the facts, understand the origins of these behaviours, accept the reality to overcome them to live a healthier and happier life, and, more importantly, not repeat the vicious ill cycle with our children.

These realisations are the main motor behind this Book; I have to take action and find solutions to all the psychological and physical trauma I was left with. Now, I was a mum myself, and I was terrified to see some horrifying unconscious signs of abuse in myself towards my children. Realising this was a massive wake-up call for me, I had to investigate and find the solution as I did not want my children to suffer or go through what I went through.

Since then, what I have learned over the last couple of years has allowed me to grow as I have never had before, and I learned so much about myself that it felt like I was being given a chance to start again. The knowledge and understanding I now had made me feel empowered and capable of taking control of my well-being, recovery, and healing in every way, but more importantly, I am ready to share my experience with everyone who is going through or has gone through similar events in their lives hoping to help understand and heal the wounds, overcome, and ultimately live a whole and happy life feeling empowered to heal the past and break free.

In the pages of this Book, I aim to provide information and an analysis of the different profiles of toxic personalities. It intends to provide you with tools to recognise these signs in the people around you. We will analyse their behaviour and the reason behind these behaviours. We will also learn how to cope with these abusers if we still have a relationship with them and if we have decided to cut all contact. We will know clear steps to start our healing and recovery process, and probably the most important legacy of this Book is to *stand up to psychological trauma to break the cycle.*

Because at the end of the day, we deserve to live a whole and happy life, we cannot be expected to take responsibility for things that happened to our parents in their childhood, nor for the experiences they have gone through. We should not be obligated to live their unlived lives. The harrowing experiences they may have gone through while growing up have marked their lives and behaviours, and it is out of our hands to fix that. If we try to do this, we risk repeating the vicious circle by allowing the ill behaviour to repeat.

Realising and accepting these is very empowering and liberating. Whatever happened to emotionally immature, narcissistic, and toxic parents is not our fault or responsibility. We cannot allow these to shape our lives.

Healing the past is a journey through the complex, often painful, yet ultimately empowering process of confronting and overcoming the legacy of a tumultuous upbringing. It's a book for those who have felt the suffocating weight of the past, which was marked by parents who couldn't provide the emotional nourishment needed to flourish.

My intention with this book is to acknowledge the wounds and discover the strength within you to heal them. Within your hands, you are holding a resource that will help you understand the intricate web of emotions, behaviours, and thought patterns that are the legacy of emotionally immature and abusive parents.

In these pages, I will share some personal experiences; through these stories, and with the help of expert insights and practical exercises, we will learn how to break free from the patterns that have held us back for far too long.

Remember, healing is not a destination but a journey that begins with the courage to confront the past and ends with the liberation of your authentic self. It's about finding your voice, reclaiming your power, and rewriting your life story. I hope this book is your companion on that transformative journey.

So, if you've ever questioned whether overcoming the shadows of your past is possible, the answer is a resounding "yes." The journey may be challenging, but it is one worth embarking upon. As you turn the page, you're taking the first step towards a brighter, more emotionally fulfilling future—a future that is truly yours to create.

Remember that healing from the impact of emotionally immature and abusive parents is a process that can take time. It's essential to seek professional help, such as therapy or counselling, to assist you. Building a support network of friends and loved ones who understand and support your journey can be immensely helpful, but one thing is sure: it's a roadmap to freedom, a guide to forging a brighter, healthier future.

CHAPTER 1 STEP 1

Am I being abused?

Defining and understanding these behaviours

E*motional Immaturity:* Emotional immaturity refers to a state in which an individual's emotional responses and coping mechanisms are underdeveloped or lag behind their chronological age. It sets apart people with difficulties in managing and healthily expressing emotions. Emotionally immature individuals may struggle with self-regulation, interpersonal relationships, empathy, and problem-solving. They often exhibit behaviours associated with emotional impulsivity, self-centeredness, and a limited capacity to understand and navigate complex emotional situations. Emotional immaturity can impact personal relationships, decision-making, and overall well-being.

Abuse: Abuse is the deliberate and harmful mistreatment, coercion, or exploitation of another person, often resulting in physical, emotional, psychological, or sexual harm. These can be in family dynamics, intimate relationships, workplaces, or within institutions. It can take different forms, such as physical abuse (inflicting bodily harm or injury), emotional or psychological abuse (manipulation, belittling, control), verbal abuse (threats, insults, humiliation), sexual abuse (unwanted sexual advances or activities without consent), and neglect (failure to provide necessary care or support). Abuse is a violation of an individual's rights, dignity, and safety, and it can have severe and long-lasting consequences on the victim's physical and mental health. It is considered a legal and social concern, often requiring intervention, support, and prevention efforts to protect individuals from harm.

Toxicity, what does it mean?

The term "toxic" describes something harmful, damaging, or detrimental to the well-being, health, or environment of an individual, group, or system. Toxicity can refer to physical, chemical, emotional, or psychological harm. In various contexts, toxicity is applied to substances, behaviours, relationships, environments, or attitudes that have the potential to cause damage, disrupt the balance, or negatively impact the overall quality of life. We can also define a toxic person as someone incapable of dealing with their traumas without affecting everybody else around them. They feel the need for negativity and conflict and find it difficult to be happy and even more difficult to see anyone else happy around them. In other words, if your relationship with your parents or any other person leaves you feeling drained, exhausted, and insecure, you may be dealing with someone with a toxic personality disorder. To help you spot these people, I list below some behaviours to look for when dealing with them.

- These individuals find it challenging to consider other people's feelings and needs.

- They rarely apologise, and if they do, it is never honest, and they tend to do this in front of other people to gain their sympathy.

- Drama is part of their life constantly, and they are not willing to do anything to change.

- They use gaslighting and passive aggression to coerce you into doing what they want.

- They do not compromise or take responsibility for their actions.

- They don't respect your boundaries and manipulate you to get what they want.

- They believe that rules and sometimes the law do not apply to them.

- They are capable of creating so much anxiety and stress to the point that this could affect you on so many levels.

- They think they are always right and belittle your values and beliefs.

Emotionally immature people: They have low empathy, don't show much respect for other people's thoughts and opinions, are preoccupied and egocentric, and have low-stress tolerance levels. In a nutshell, if the person you are dealing with always expects you to help them but is never there for you, if they drain your energy and interacting with them makes you feel down. You think your general well-being is impacted negatively. If this is the case, you can be sure you are dealing with a toxic person, and you need to take action to gain control of your life and not be affected by them.

These are some reasons why it is essential to learn about these personality disorders and deal with any issues that these experiences may have left in us.

Recognising the signs and patterns

In this section, we will look at all the different types of emotionally immature and toxic personalities to get new insights into our parent's behaviour and our relationships, enabling us to control the situation.

There are many types of toxic personalities, but some of the most prominent are the emotionally immature, controlling/ manipulative, narcissistic, and sociopath. In this section, we will analyse each type to gain perspective and understanding and potentially equip ourselves with the knowledge to identify and cope with these personality types in the people around us.

The emotionally immature type:

What is an emotionally immature person?

First, it is essential to establish what emotional maturity is. We can define this as understanding that we may not be able to control or change people and situations around us; however, we can prevent ourselves and how we react to and deal with these situations. Emotionally immature people do not have this capability.

On the contrary, an emotionally immature parent has a low-stress tolerance, does not take accountability for any situation, and instead likes to blame others. They are very self-involved and susceptible and have low empathy for everyone else. They tend to pay attention to the physical needs of their children, dismissing their emotional needs completely; they often are single-minded, finding it offensive if other people have different ideas. They could be killjoys and quick to react with intense but shallow emotions.

As a consequence of these relationships, you could feel guilty or unhappy, lack confidence, and have difficulty trusting your instincts. Being conscious of other people's feelings can make you think you must care for them. The danger here is that you could feel lonely, betrayed, angry, or abandoned altogether. These are the very reasons why it is essential to acknowledge and understand these behaviours.

Emotionally chaotic parents: they are at the top of the emotional scale as they cannot control their emotions, causing anxiety in their children as they are unpredictable and often unstable. As adults, they could be overly aware of other people's needs to the detriment of their own.

The driven parent: these gold-obsessed, pushy parents can only focus on their children's achievements, forgetting or ignoring their children's needs and feelings. They always ask and demand more, paying hardly any attention to the emotional connection with their children. This behaviour could make the children insecure as adults, thinking they have never done enough, leading them to complicated psychological and mental health issues.

Passive or hand-off parents: these individuals take the easy-going approach to avoid conflict or challenging situations. At first, they seem more emotionally available to the children but fall short when providing structure and guidance. These children grow up thinking they must protect themselves and their parents as they see them as vulnerable adults.

Rejecting parents: these emotionally immature parents want nothing to do with their children. They only interact with the family to issue orders or express their anger. Children growing up under these circumstances find it difficult to express themselves or ask for things as they feel they are being a nuisance or bothering people. They could need more confidence to speak or stand up for themselves.

Where is emotional immaturity rooted?

Sometimes, these behaviours could be a *Product of childhood emotional neglect.* In this case, we can see these families drawing a curtain on painful and difficult situations to avoid facing any emotions; they do not know how to recognise, express, share or cope with their emotions. These individuals will grow up not knowing how to handle their feelings. They will find it very difficult to deal with situations where they are emotionally compromised.

Recovery for these individuals is very achievable, as they can increase their emotional maturity by paying attention to their own emotions, acknowledging how they work, and learning to become mindful of them. These processes may be longer for some people than for others, but they can be accomplished.

The controlling type

It is very typical that, as humans, we like to control our lives and the things that happen around us. We must be in control of our actions to be aware of the repercussions these could have on other people. However, we feel uncomfortable when other people are not doing what we want or find it difficult to let them make their own mistakes. In that case, this is when controlling behaviour becomes very harmful, as it undermines the ability of the person to think and decide for themselves, and it jeopardises their freedom. We can all choose what is best for us and make our own mistakes.

It is essential to be aware that controlling people have co-dependency issues and excessive psychological and emotional reliance on others. They need to control everything and everyone around them to feel happier and better about themselves. Below, I will highlight some of the most prominent characteristics of a controlling person.

They are inflexible; it is their way or no way, and they need the ability to adjust to different circumstances, ideas, or situations. Authoritarian individuals are typically rigid, steadfast in their beliefs or positions, and unwilling or unable to consider alternative approaches or perspectives.

They are not interested in anyone's opinion, as they believe what they think is what should be done.

They do not like you to question them, and they get distraught if you do, as they want you to follow them without question. They cannot adapt and are never open to suggestions from anyone.

These are some of the tools used by controlling people to make us feel insecure so they can manipulate us; they could be so convincing in their ways that you end up thinking they indeed know better.

They are **highly critical;** in their eyes, there will always be a better way for you to do things, and they will imply that they could have done it better themselves. If you have achieved something at work or school, they will ask why you have only just done this or why you are not the number one at it. This scenario creates a feeling of inferiority, which they take full advantage of to have more control over you.

It is **never their fault;** it is always somebody else's. They convince themselves they know best and that you are wrong to shift the blame on you. They like to make us believe by telling us directly that we should do what they say or, even more, what they want.

They need to be the **centre of attention** and will always try to find a way to turn situations to themselves. To achieve this, they try to **make rules for everybody else's lives** so they can control what we do and who we see and will try to stop us if they believe who we see is a threat to them and their ideas for us.

When you finally start to be yourself again and gain control of your life, **they will try to make you feel bad about it**. They will tell you and everyone else how much you have changed and are not who you used to be, implying that you have changed for the worse. My mother tried to convince everyone in the family that I was an evil daughter, that I had become a challenging person to live with, and that I was making her suffer a lot. All because I was starting to become my person again.

With time, all these could make you feel worthless and could make you believe that your opinions do not count, which could lead to deep psychological trauma. It took me several sessions of hypnosis and a load of personal psychological mindfulness as an adult to express and defend myself in all sorts of different environments and situations.

However, it is essential to know and understand that in most cases, people have become controlling because of their own experiences in life, as they may have gone through challenging situations that were totally out of their control and had to experience pain, loneliness, and total neglect as a result of these, so being in control makes them feel safe. We will analyse this better in future chapters.

The narcissist

Narcissists are very arrogant people with a massive sense of entitlement, are very superficial, and genuinely believe they are unique individuals. They have a pathological need for attention and validation and cannot empathise with anyone. They live in a fantasy world where they are the centre of attention.

Within this are a few different patterns of narcissism, and the first one I like to talk about is the ***Malignant or toxic narcissist***. These individuals are the most challenging to deal with as they tend to be very charismatic and well-liked people on the outside. When you first meet them, they have high self-esteem and no issues acting openly with superiority. However, they have no problem exploiting and manipulating people around them; they take advantage of the system to get or do what they want, cheat, and lie without remorse. They are dangerous as they believe they are entitled to everything and know everything. They could get outraged if anyone contradicts them and will set out to destroy you if you stand in their way; they are manipulative and mean. As Dr. Les Carter would say, they have an underdeveloped conscience.

The following type I would like to talk of the ***grandiose narcissist***, also known as the ***classic narcissist.*** They only care about themselves and cannot put themselves in anybody else's shoes. They expect to be recognised and awarded consistently, enjoy boasting about anything they do, cannot accept criticism, and avoid embarrassment. They are very pretentious and cannot cope with the idea of anybody being more successful than they are. They monopolise conversations, fantasise about power and success, and exaggerate all their achievements. They refuse to give up control but do not take responsibility. Unfortunately, they have no problem crossing other people's boundaries.

The other pattern of narcissism is the ***covert or vulnerable narcissist***. Whilst these people share many of the same traits as the *overt classic narcissist*, they tend to be more insecure, self-conscious, and introverted. They are *susceptible to criticism*; what everybody thinks of them is extremely important, but they often pretend that the complaint is not addressed to them and, on the inside, are deeply affected by it. They tend to use *passive aggression* to attack back, and they do this because they very sincerely believe they are unique and, therefore, superior and entitled to get what they want. Jealousy is a trademark of these personalities who want to get back at someone who has more success than they have. In the workplace, they will do this in blame-shifting or procrastination as they believe they are too unique or superior for their job.

In conclusion, these people suffer depression, anxiety, and envy; they believe they are undiscovered geniuses, nobody understands them, and the world has not given them the place they deserve.

The last pattern of narcissism I would like to talk about is ***communal narcissism***; this is that typical social media activist who enjoys all the charitable work for the attention and recognition this brings them. They enjoy making themselves look like a *Martyr*; they only *show concern for social needs in public* where everybody can see them. They genuinely believe they are the best ones to perform the task at hand and enjoy overdramatised situations or events to attract more attention to themselves. In conclusion, they use communal means to satisfy their need for grandiosity.

There are a few essential things to consider when dealing with narcissistic people, and establishing *clear boundaries* and *staying assertive* when it comes to getting them to respect you and your space are the more important ones. They must know you are unprepared to accept their self-centred behaviour in your space. It is also vital to *stay true to your beliefs* and not let them dictate what you should do or how you should feel or think. These people will try to convince you to do what they want so that you serve their purpose.

Do not try to confront them about their behaviour; this will only infuriate them as they cannot recognise this or accept any criticism, and they will start attacking you, perhaps by using some gaslighting techniques to make you feel bad, guilty, or responsible for the situation. Recognising and accepting that these people will not change, and that limiting interaction is the best solution to deal with them is fundamental.

Narcissistic parents can make decisions that could hurt their kids not because they are unaware of what they are doing but because they do not care about anybody else but themselves.

The sociopath

The sociopath is undoubtedly one of the most challenging and dangerous antisocial personality disorders, as it encompasses many of the toxic personality traits we previously spoke about; plus, they are happy to control and manipulate people and comfortable breaking the rules or even the law to get what they want. Analysing the characteristics of a sociopath can help us to recognise these in the people around us.

Lack of empathy: The main characteristic of a sociopath is that they feel little or no remorse for things they have done or damage or hurts they have caused to others, as they genuinely see people as a means to an end. These individuals cannot put themselves in someone else's shoes, which will make it impossible for them to understand other people's feelings, and therefore, do not feel any guilt or remorse when they cause pain to others. We may see these individuals as calm in extreme situations, not because they can control themselves more than others but because they lack empathy. They genuinely see themselves as superior to others and are entitled to everything they desire.

They *lack intimacy*, making it very difficult to establish and maintain a relationship with anyone. Sociopaths tend to be very lonely and only engage in relationships to exploit, coerce, deceive, or dominate others for their benefit. They can come across as charismatic and charming, but this will always be to win people to manipulate and use them. They are highly ambitious and take any opportunity to get what they want without regard for anybody around them.

Sociopaths tend to be involved in *reckless and criminal behaviour*. They are very impulsive and aggressive and act without considering the consequences, resulting in situations detrimental to anyone around them, including themselves.

Finally, I would like to point out that a sociopath has very similar personality traits to a psychopath. Still, there are some significant differences, and I consider the following some of the most important.

Sociopaths act without thinking and genuinely don't care about others, whilst psychopaths plan every move they make and pretend to care about others.

Sociopaths are a product of the environment as it is believed that this develops due to psychological trauma from childhood, whilst psychopaths are born like that; in other words, their condition is genetic.

The generational cycle: How it perpetuates

The generational cycle of abuse is a complex phenomenon in which patterns of abusive behaviour, whether physical, emotional, or psychological, are passed down from one generation to the next within a family or social context. Unfortunately, as humans, we seem to imitate negative behaviours very quickly, which is deeply concerning as it is the cause for these behaviours being perpetuated.

It is essential to analyse why we can perpetuate these cycles.

Learned Behaviour: Children often learn behaviours, attitudes, and coping mechanisms from their parents or caregivers. Suppose they grow up in an abusive environment. In that case, they may view abusive behaviours as normal or acceptable ways of interacting with others. This *normalisation* occurs when abusive behaviour is so pervasive in a family that it becomes ingrained in daily life. Children may witness abuse between their parents or directed at themselves, leading them to believe this is how relationships function. They will apply this same principle everywhere they go; this is how we see these behaviours carried to the workplace.

Lack of Healthy Role Models: Abusive households lack healthy role models for communication, conflict resolution, and emotional regulation. In these situations, we can see children replicating abusive patterns they have observed without positive examples. It is also essential to talk about *Emotional Scars;* abusive experiences can leave deep emotional scars on victims, manifesting as unresolved trauma, anger, resentment, or feelings of powerlessness. When these traumas are unresolved, and individuals do not receive the necessary support for healing, they may carry these emotional wounds into adulthood, potentially perpetuating the cycle and affecting their mental and physical health. Research has shown that autoimmune diseases are linked closely to psychological trauma.

The interplay of Power and Control: Power and control imbalances often characterise abusive dynamics. The abuser exerts power over the victim, making ***breaking free*** from the cycle challenging. Victims may later become abusers themselves to regain a sense of control. Abusive behaviour is more likely to persist if it goes unaddressed or unchallenged; this can happen when family members or society fail to recognise the signs of abuse or take action to protect the victims.

Trauma Bonds: Victims of abuse may form complex emotional bonds or co-dependency with their abusers due to a phenomenon known as "trauma bonding." This bond can make it difficult for victims to leave abusive relationships or break the cycle. *Social and Cultural Factors* can also play a role in perpetuating the generational cycle of abuse. Stigma, shame, lack of resources, and cultural norms can all contribute to silence and inaction in abusive situations.

Breaking the generational cycle of abuse is challenging but an essential endeavour. It requires a multi-faceted approach. Let's talk about these below.

Education and Awareness: Awareness of the signs of abuse and its effects is crucial. Healthy relationships and conflict resolution education can help individuals recognise and avoid abusive behaviours. Therapy and counselling can also help individuals who have experienced abuse heal from their trauma and develop healthier coping strategies.

Intervention and Support: Early intervention and support for victims are critical. Some things include access to counselling, therapy, and safe shelters for those escaping abusive situations. We can also talk about *legal protection,* which is the legal measures to hold abusers accountable for their actions and ensure the safety of victims. Communities and social services should provide resources like hotlines, support groups, and counselling to help individuals escape abusive environments.

Promotion of Healthy Relationships: Healthy relationships, communication skills, and conflict resolution techniques can equip individuals with the tools to build respectful and non-abusive connections with others. Breaking the generational cycle of abuse requires a collective effort from society, individuals, and institutions. It demands empathy, awareness, and a commitment to creating environments where abuse is not tolerated, and healing and support are readily available for survivors.

The impact on children's development

Abuse, whether it is physical, emotional, psychological, or sexual, can have profound and lasting impacts on a child's development. These effects can manifest across various domains of a child's life and persist into adulthood.

Emotional and Psychological Impact:

Children who experience abuse may develop low self-esteem and a negative self-image. They may internalise feelings of shame and worthlessness, which could lead to anxiety and Depression. They may struggle with overwhelming feelings of fear, sadness, or hopelessness. They may experience intense mood swings, anger, or emotional numbness due to difficulty regulating their emotions. However, this will take many proactive and mindful approaches to overcome.

Cognitive Impact: The chronic stress and trauma associated with abuse can impair cognitive functioning, including memory, attention, and problem-solving skills. Children who experience abuse may have lower academic achievement due to mental challenges and emotional distress.

Social Impact:

Difficulty in Forming Relationships: Abused children may struggle with forming healthy, trusting relationships with peers and adults. They may have trouble establishing boundaries and trusting others. These situations could lead to isolation and withdrawal, and some children isolate themselves as a coping mechanism to protect themselves from further harm. Aggressive behaviour is also typical in cases of children who experienced abuse. They may exhibit aggressive behaviour towards others due to anger and frustration.

Physical Health Impact: Abuse can lead to physical health problems due to stress, neglect, or direct physical harm. These health issues may persist into adulthood. Also, some abused children may engage in self-harming behaviours to cope with emotional pain. Speech, Language, and Motor Skill Delays: Abused children may experience speech and language delays, especially if exposed to a traumatic environment from a young age and may experience delays in developing motor skills in neglect or physical abuse cases.

Long-Term Consequences: Adult Mental Health Issues: The impact of abuse can extend into adulthood, leading to mental health issues such as post-traumatic stress disorder (PTSD), borderline personality disorder (BPD), and substance abuse. Not to forget the long-term effect of psychological trauma on our health that can sometimes lead to other illnesses in adulthood. Without intervention and healing, some survivors of child abuse may perpetuate the cycle of abuse in their relationships and families.

It is important to note that the impact of abuse can vary widely depending on factors such as the type and severity of abuse, the duration, and the presence of protective factors like a supportive caregiver or access to therapy. Early intervention, treatment, and a safe, nurturing environment can mitigate some of the adverse effects of abuse and promote healing and resilience in children. Recognising and addressing child abuse sooner rather than later is crucial to protecting a child's physical and emotional well-being and allowing them to heal, thrive and grow in a safe and loving environment.

CHAPTER 2 STEP 2

Analysing the child inside

Understanding Emotionally Immature and Abusive Parents.

Understanding:

Most memories I have of myself growing up are of feeling on edge, frightened, and worried that I may upset my parents, as I knew they would have severely punished me if I did anything slightly wrong.

My parents took pride in having a collection of punishment tools and used them. Depending on ***"how badly we behaved"****,* they will choose the plaited cable or the buckle end of my father's belt. They had the idea that making their children frightened of them was a way of gaining respect from them. From a very young age, I felt angry about how they treated my brother and me to the point that sometimes I wanted to report them, tell someone, or show my teachers the bruises and wounds. What they were doing was wrong. But of course, most children my age were suffering from similar experiences at that time, so it made people believe that it was all fine; that was how you raise children.

Now, one of the most important reasons for me to write this book is that despite all those experiences and being so against it, there is a very high chance of repeating these behaviours and carry on with the ill cycle of abuse. Not because we consciously wanted to do it but because it is what we know and is in our subconscious

One afternoon, I went to pick my daughter up from school; she was about eight years old, and honestly, I don't remember why. Still, I remember being cross with her, grabbing her by the hair, and shaking her. I was horrified at what I had done minutes after. My daughter is a lovely girl, but even if she was not, no reason justifies me to do what I have done; this was a massive wake-up call as I realised what had happened to me in my childhood had left me with an intense scare; there were severe issues with my behaviour and something that needed immediate attention. Suddenly, **I could see that I was acting like my mother, all the things I always hated about her. I was starting to do it myself. I needed to deal with it; it needed to stop, and I needed to find help.**

When we grow up with these experiences, we will inevitably act the same way and repeat these with our children unless we deal with the traumas. It will come out when we least expected it and from nowhere; this is why I consider this step super important;

looking into our parents' past, the experiences they have gone through, and the marks that these would have left on them is fundamental. Analysing and understanding these would allow us to better comprehend their behaviour and deal with the legacy they would have left on us. In some cases, it will help us to heal the hurt caused by these.

Childhood trauma. How can it affect us?

Childhood trauma is a child's exposure to events that would have been very distressing and damaging. These traumatic events could include domestic violence, sexual, physical, or verbal abuse, separation from a parent, or emotional and physical neglect. An intrusive medical procedure, a dangerous accident, or a natural disaster, like a tsunami or a hurricane, could also be a traumatic event that could leave an emotional or psychological scar on any individual. Anything frightening or threatening a child's or adult's physical and mental integrity is a trauma.

Analysing these elements is fundamental as they will give us answers to many questions we had, not just in regard to our traumas but that of our parents, as all these events can have a long-lasting impact on our lives and could be the root of our parent's toxic and abusive behaviour toward us. They can lead to other psychological disorders, like anxiety or depression, disturbing our minds, beliefs, and values. More dangerously, these events can profoundly affect our biological health throughout our lifetime.

When I was about ten, my mother sent me to the shop to buy some provisions. The store was approximately 1 mile from my house; she gave me what would have been the equivalent of £10 and a list of things she wanted me to buy. I set off happily for the store, but when I arrived, I realised I had lost the money on my way. Panic struck as I knew that my mother would not be happy, and that severe punishment was inevitable. I had no choice; I had to come back and tell my mother that I could not get anything she asked for and that I had lost the money on the way to the store.

Indeed, what I received was a hideous and painful physical punishment. Still, this time, my mother thought that it would be a good lesson for me to learn to embarrass me so I would never repeat this incident. So immediately after, she hit me, and before I could recover from it, she went to her draw and took out the little pair of golden earrings that my father had given me when I was a little girl and sent me to the neighbour across the road to sell it for the £10 I have just lost.

That event left me deeply psychologically scared. I am unsure if I learned anything that day, but I never forgot.

For many years, I questioned this behaviour. I often blamed myself for it, thinking that my mother was right and that I must have been a very *"problematic girl"*, as she used to call me. Sometimes, I secretly looked for help. *I remember standing in the school's playground the day after I had received punishment from my parents, thinking that if I lifted my skirt, one of the teachers could see my wounds and bruises and might be able to help me.* I was in the early years of primary school then, and I remember thinking what was happening to me was wrong. It could not have been right!

Only many years later, when I realised that there was much more to my mother's behaviour than what could be seen, I recognised that the problem was deeply rooted elsewhere and not with me, as she always made me believe.

She was very resentful of the experiences she had gone through in her childhood; the abandonment from her mother was something that she always talked about. She would get irate when talking about it, and it often felt that she blamed us, her children, for her experiences. She never spoke to her mother about it.

At this point, the questioning started. Why was my mother like that? There was so much spitefulness and hate in her behaviour most of the time. I had carried this massive burden of guilt and responsibility for many years and needed answers. I have to understand why.

Looking into the reason for these behaviours

Looking into this was like opening Pandora's box for the first time. There was so much psychological trauma, hurt, and many things that needed to be dealt with and, consequently, many potential reasons for my mother's behaviour. When dealing with these within our immediate circle, information is fundamental to help us understand and deal with the issues, overcome them, find answers, and heal.

Childhood neglect is one of the first causes of abusive and toxic adult behaviour. Let us start by defining ***neglect in childhood*** as an extreme omission by the parents or caregiver towards a child, where they deprive the child of fundamental physical, emotional, or psychological needs that could result in physical or mental harm.

Neglect can come in many forms; some of these can be a failure to provide medical care, education, or shelter, failure to provide appropriate clothing and nourishment, as well as a lack of emotional and psychological support or supervision, making abandonment the worse form of neglect but unfortunately one of the most common child maltreatments.

At his point, I would like to point out that this physical and psychological neglect is most commonly attended to, possibly because they are more visible or familiar. Still, emotional neglect could also cause serious mental health issues in adulthood. These individuals had all their physical needs met as a child but lacked emotional support from their parents or caregivers.

Poor self-discipline, anger and aggressive behaviour, depression, eating disorders, guilt and shame, and post-traumatic stress disorder are some of the consequences of emotional neglect in childhood.

Anybody who has suffered these forms of childhood neglect is likelier to become an emotionally immature adult, a narcissist, or even a sociopath.

My mother is the second child of 9 children born in a very humble family in the countryside of Paraguay, South America. My grandmother believed that giving her children away to families in a better financial situation was a good thing to do, so every single one of her children was sent away to be looked after by strangers, my mother in between them.

She was only six years of age when she was sent away for the first time to live with a family who were her godparents and were supposed to care for her. My mother told us that she was treated like a servant when she arrived at the house. At six years old, she was expected to clean the house, wash the dishes, and do the laundry (they did not have washing machines at those times, so she had to wash it all by hand). Her carers would have punished my mother if the job was not done correctly. As a little girl, she lost all sense of time and did not know how long she was there or when she would see her mother again.

I always remember the event she told me and my brothers several times of her being very ill with what sounded like it could have been chickenpox, sitting on the floor under the hot sun doing the laundry by hand, and feeling very unwell, when she saw my grandmother walking into the gate and feeling very relieved at her mother's sight.

I don't know how long would have passed from the moment she arrived at that house to the day she was sat on the floor under the hot sun, ill with high temperature, washing the clothes by hand, and what other abuse she may have gone through in that house. In other words, my grandmother left her 6-year-old daughter in the hands of those people, but it was enough to leave a significant mark on my mother.

Let's talk about ***Emotional immaturity;*** as mentioned before, we can call this the inability to take responsibility for our feelings and not control our reactions to the point that our actions are unpredictable and unreliable. This struggle with our emotional reactions creates a sense of insecurity and anxiety in the people around us, especially our children. Being a child of an emotionally immature parent is highly unsettling, as our parents are the first ones meant to give us stability and a sense of safety. These are qualities that emotionally immature parents did not experience growing up; therefore, they find it challenging to provide these to their children as they may not even be aware of them; this is why looking into our parents' past and analysing ours is fundamental to finding answers to the problems. Or we could end up in a vicious circle as emotionally immature parenting could result in emotionally neglected children, bringing more complicated psychological issues such as *low self-esteem.* The parent's lack of affection and validation could result in a *negative self-view*.

These experiences could lead us to enter unhealthy and abusive relationships where we do not expect much as we grow up believing that all intimate relationships are toxic and have unhealthy dynamics, so screaming, overreacting, affection withdrawal and physical violence are part of any relationship; this is when we can become *people pleasers* to gain validation and "love" from the people around us, or like it was in my case, I was simply wholly blocked. I could not speak up, defend myself, or express myself in simple words. I clearly remember the first time it happened, and for the first time, I thought something was wrong with me.

As a young girl, I belonged to a Christian organisation that helped and supported young people from deprived backgrounds. I spent my weekends travelling around my country, meeting other young people like me, and I enjoyed doing this. I found it comforting being with these people as these activities fundamentally kept me out of my parent's house, out of my mother's sight, and out of any argument. Thinking back on it, I now remember spending a load of time with friends as it was an escape from my parent's house. Anyway, I clearly remember being present at a meeting of this organisation and entirely against what was being discussed but unable to speak up or express my point of view or what I thought or felt about it. I just burst into tears because I could not speak or understand why. With time, this worsened and started affecting other areas of my life. As I grew and needed to express myself or make decisions, my emotions got the best of me. I took several sessions with a hypnotherapist and plenty of auto-psychoanalysis to overcome that blockage.

When the book Emotional Intelligence by Daniel Goleman was published in 1995, I was 20 years old and an absolute emotional mess. I was still living in my parents' house in Paraguay because in Paraguay, a child, especially a girl, only leaves the maternal house dressed in white the day they get married. I remember the tremendous amount of publicity for the book launch. It even attracted my mother's attention as she thought it could be the perfect book for her emotionally unintelligent daughter. At the time, I thought that was just one more label she was putting on me. Still, she was undoubtedly correct in saying I was not very intelligent regarding my emotions. The only issue was that she did not see, understand, or admit the origin of the emotional mess. Unfortunately, it would take me many more years to recognise it, understand it, and look to heal from it, and to be honest, I am still working on that today. **Childhood trauma** let's analyse this a bit further. As we mentioned, being subject to **abuse and neglect** and living in a **chaotic, violent, and unstable** family environment are significant causes of psychological trauma that we take to adulthood. Also, children who have experienced **homelessness or poverty** will undoubtedly have some psychological scare in their personalities.

Traumatic events will undoubtedly significantly impact our mental health. As we said before, these are the direct causes of toxic behaviour in adulthood. Individuals who grow up in unstable environments surrounded by unreliable people often question if anybody loves them or cares for them, but this is not always at a conscious level. We often see these people live their lives with their stress response constantly activated, which is detrimental to their physical and mental health in the long term; this is when antisocial personality disorders like narcissism and sociopath can be rooted, as unconsciously they will try to find different ways to protect themselves sometimes by believing that they are superior, hold the truth and are right about everything (cows are green, not black and white or brown) and everyone else is wrong.

These individuals have gone through experiences where they had their pride, confidence, and self-belief shattered, so these toxic behaviours become like a defence mechanism to survive.

The psychological scar that my mother ended up with from her mother's abandonment has marked her for life. Unfortunately, she was and is so deeply traumatised by those experiences that she never overcame them. Still, she never had access to enough information to help her overcome these traumas. No one did in those times; they have conditioned her life until today, and it will probably not change. My grandmother is a hard woman who likely did not receive care and attention from her mother either. So again, we see the vicious cycle repeating itself.

Not long after my grandmother brought my six-year-old mother back to the family home, she was sent again to live with another family, and that happened again until she was an adult. In between my grandmother's lack of care and affection and all the experiences my mother went through at the hands of those strangers, I can confidently say that my mother was not taught or shown how to care for someone, so she never learned what it was like to be loved and watched for.

It is also essential to look into the ***family history*** for *antisocial personality disorders* or other *mental illnesses,* such as ***depression*** *or anxiety*, as these would have had a massive impact on building the personalities.

Analysing these factors is highly important for adult children dealing with emotionally immature, toxic, and abusive parents, as understanding will help overcome trauma caused by these experiences and heal.

In conclusion, we can safely say that toxic behaviour is usually born from childhood abuse or trauma. It is a profound and complicated psychological issue that the affected person is not always aware of. Their behaviour is a defence mechanism and ensures no one abuses them again. This behaviour is not something they are conscious of most of the time.

Empathy

Empathy is a powerful and transformative force that can play a significant role in healing the wounds caused by an emotionally immature and abusive parent; it can serve as a great instrument in the healing process:

Why Is It Important:

Empathy validates the survivor's feelings and experiences. When someone acknowledges and understands the pain and suffering caused by an abusive parent, it sends a powerful message that their emotions are valid and deserving of attention. ***Empathy creates an***

emotional connection between the survivor and a compassionate listener or supporter. This connection fosters trust and a sense of safety, essential for healing. Survivors of abuse often feel isolated and alone. Empathy reminds them that they are not alone and that others care about their well-being.

Healing from Shame: Abuse can lead to feelings of shame and self-blame. Empathy helps survivors challenge these negative beliefs and replace them with self-compassion and self-acceptance. Sharing one's experiences with an empathetic listener can be cathartic. It provides an opportunity to release pent-up emotions, a crucial step in the healing journey.

How Empathy Can Help in Healing:

Empathetic individuals practice *active listening*, which involves giving full attention to the survivor's story without judgment or interruption. This non-judgmental space allows survivors to express their emotions openly. Empathetic individuals validate survivors' feelings by acknowledging their pain and suffering. Offering support can include providing resources, suggesting therapy or counselling, or simply being there as a source of comfort. Empathetic individuals help survivors practice self-compassion by reminding them they deserve love, care, and understanding, just like anyone else.

Empathy empowers survivors by encouraging them to share their experiences and take control of their healing journey. It helps them recognise their resilience and strength. Developing trust is crucial for survivors who may have experienced broken trust in abusive relationships. Empathetic support can help rebuild trust in others and the healing process. Empathy can give survivors a new perspective on their experiences. It allows them to see that not all relationships or interactions are abusive and that there is hope for healthier connections.

Encouraging survivors to express their thoughts and emotions through talking, writing, or art can be therapeutic and healing. Empathy supports these forms of self-expression and helps survivors reframe their life narrative from victimhood to resilience and growth. It enables them to see themselves as survivors rather than just victims. The empathetic presence of others can *create a safe and nurturing environment* where survivors can explore their feelings, memories, and pain without fear of judgment or rejection.

In summary, empathy is vital to healing from the wounds caused by an emotionally immature and abusive parent. It provides validation, emotional connection, and a safe space for survivors to express themselves, confront their pain, and begin the journey toward recovery and transformation. Whether received from a therapist, friend, or support group, empathy is crucial in healing, rebuilding their lives, and finding hope for healthier relationships.

Breaking the Silence

The power of acknowledging the past

Acknowledging and addressing past abuse can be an essential and empowering step in a survivor's healing process. Some reasons why this is important and how it can empower us for the future, as we stated before, are *Validation of Feelings*: Acknowledging the past abuse validates the survivor's feelings and experiences. It allows them to recognise that what they went through was accurate and harmful. This validation can be a decisive step towards healing as it helps survivors understand their pain is legitimate. *Breaking the Silence*: Many abuse survivors carry a heavy burden of secrecy and shame. Acknowledging the past abuse is a way of breaking the silence and secrecy surrounding abuse; this can reduce feelings of isolation and loneliness, as survivors may find support and understanding from others who have had similar experiences.

Reclaiming Personal Power

Confronting the past abuse empowers survivors to take control of their narrative and their lives. It shifts the focus from being a victim to being a survivor. It can help individuals regain a sense of personal power and agency over their own lives. *Understanding Patterns*: Acknowledging past abuse can help survivors understand how it may have affected their behaviours, beliefs, and relationships. This self-awareness can be a foundation for making positive changes in one's life and breaking unhealthy patterns that may have developed due to the abuse. *Seeking Healing and Support*: Once abuse has been acknowledged, survivors can seek the necessary support and resources for healing; this might include therapy, support groups, or counselling. *Preventing Future Abuse*: By recognising past abuse, survivors can become more aware of potential red flags in relationships and situations. This awareness can help them make informed choices to protect themselves from future abuse.

Advocacy and Empowerment: Some survivors use their experiences to advocate for change, raise awareness about abuse, or support others who have been through similar situations. Acknowledging the past can be a catalyst for activism and helping others. It's important to note that recognising past abuse is a deeply personal and often challenging process. Survivors should seek support from trusted friends, family, therapists, or support groups as they navigate this journey. Healing is not linear, and taking as much time as needed to come to terms with the past is okay. Ultimately, acknowledging the past can be a decisive step towards reclaiming one's life and moving towards a healthier and more empowered future.

The emotional toll of silence

Silence is generally not beneficial for someone who has suffered from abuse, and it can be highly harmful for several reasons. It can be profound and detrimental to their mental, emotional, and physical well-being. *Emotional Suppression*: Silence often involves suppressing emotions and feelings related to the abuse. This emotional suppression can lead to increased stress, anxiety, and depression. Unresolved emotions can fester and cause ongoing psychological distress. Keeping the abuse a secret can lead to isolation and loneliness. Survivors may feel like they are the only ones going through such experiences, which can intensify feelings of shame and alienation. Isolation can further contribute to mental health issues.

Lack of Validation: When survivors cannot talk about their experiences, they may not receive the necessary validation, which is a crucial part of the healing process, and without it, survivors may feel like their feelings and experiences are not legitimate, which can worsen their emotional state. *Inhibiting Healing*: The silence surrounding abuse can inhibit the healing process. It can prevent survivors from seeking professional help, counselling, or therapy, essential for processing trauma and developing coping strategies. *Continued Vulnerability*: Silence can make survivors vulnerable to further abuse. Suppose the perpetrator is not held accountable or the abuse is not disclosed. In that case, it may continue, putting the survivor at risk of additional harm.

Negative Self-Perception

Survivors often blame themselves for the abuse or believe they did something to deserve it. This negative self-perception can persist in silence, leading to low self-esteem and self-worth. *Recurring Trauma*: Unprocessed trauma can resurface over time. Survivors may experience flashbacks, nightmares, or triggers that bring back painful memories and emotions, further exacerbating their distress. *Impact on Relationships*: The inability to talk about the abuse can strain relationships with friends and family. Survivors may withdraw from loved ones or have difficulty explaining their emotions and behaviours, leading to misunderstandings and conflicts. *Isolation*: Silence often goes hand-in-hand with isolation. Survivors may feel that they cannot or should not talk about their experiences, which can lead to a profound sense of loneliness. They may believe no one will understand or support them, leading to further isolation.

Silence can perpetuate feelings of *shame and guilt*. Survivors may blame themselves for the abuse or believe they did something to deserve it. The inability to speak about the abuse can reinforce these negative self-perceptions. Keeping the abuse a secret often involves suppressing emotions associated with the trauma. This emotional suppression can lead to various mental health issues, including anxiety, depression, and post-traumatic stress disorder (PTSD).

The silence surrounding abuse can strain relationships with friends and family. Survivors may withdraw from loved ones or struggle to explain their behaviours and emotions, leading to misunderstandings and conflicts. Silence can also erode self-esteem. Survivors may feel their experiences don't matter or are unworthy of love and support; this can lead to a negative self-image.

When survivors cannot talk about their experiences, they may feel invalidated. Validation is a crucial aspect of healing, and the absence of it can hinder recovery. Unprocessed trauma can resurface over time, leading to ongoing emotional distress and potentially triggering events or situations that remind survivors of the abuse. Silence can prevent survivors from seeking help or support. Therapy, counselling, and support groups can be essential for healing. Still, these resources may only be helpful if survivors can speak about their experiences.

It is essential to create a safe and non-judgmental environment where survivors can talk about their experiences to address the emotional toll of silence and its impact on survivors of abuse; this will encourage them to express their feelings and concerns and to seek therapy or counselling from professionals experienced in trauma and abuse. These professionals can help survivors process their emotions and develop coping strategies.

Connecting survivors with support groups or organisations specialising in helping abuse survivors will be vital. These networks can provide validation, empathy, and a sense of community where survivors can practice self-care and self-compassion. Self-care strategies can help manage the emotional toll of silence and ongoing healing.

Breaking the silence is a significant step toward healing for survivors of abuse. It can be challenging but also lead to emotional liberation, validation, and the opportunity to build a healthier, more empowered future. In summary, silence in the context of abuse can be profoundly harmful as it can perpetuate emotional suppression, isolation, and a lack of validation. It can inhibit healing, make survivors vulnerable to further harm, and contribute to ongoing mental health issues. Encouraging survivors to break the silence and seek support is crucial for their well-being and recovery. Survivors need to know that they are not alone and that resources and people are available to help them heal and move forward healthier.

Open dialogue and self-expression are significant and therapeutic for survivors of abuse. Talking about their experiences and emotions allows survivors to recognise that what they went through was real and that their feelings are legitimate. Survivors often carry a heavy burden of secrecy and shame. Open dialogue breaks the silence and secrecy surrounding abuse, reducing feelings of isolation and loneliness. It lets survivors know they are not alone and that there are people who care and want to support them.

Processing Trauma: Talking about the abuse with a therapist, counsellor, or support group can help survivors process their trauma. It provides a safe space to explore and make sense of their experiences, essential for healing. Sharing one's story can be empowering. It shifts the focus from being a victim to a survivor taking control of their narrative. It can help individuals regain a sense of personal power and agency over their own lives.

Building a Support System:

Open dialogue can lead to establishing a support system. Survivors can connect with friends, family, or support groups who can offer empathy, understanding, and guidance. These connections can be crucial for recovery as they help reduce abuse survivors' shame and guilt. Expressing their experiences can help them realise that the shame and guilt belong to the perpetrator, not them, which can liberate and improve their self-esteem.

Understanding Patterns: Talking about the abuse can help survivors understand how it may have affected their behaviours, beliefs, and relationships. This self-awareness can be the foundation for positive changes in one's life and breaking unhealthy patterns.

Advocacy and Awareness: Some survivors find healing and purpose in using their experiences to advocate for change and raise awareness about abuse. They become advocates for themselves and others who have experienced similar trauma; this is my primary tool for recovery and healing, and it is gratifying to help others by sharing my experiences.

It's important to note that open dialogue and self-expression should occur in a safe and supportive environment. Survivors may share their experiences with trusted friends, family, therapists, or support groups. Professional therapy or counselling is often recommended because trained therapists can provide guidance and support in a structured and confidential setting.

Overall, open dialogue and self-expression are potent tools for healing and recovery for abuse survivors. They can help individuals regain their voice, reclaim their agency, and move towards a healthier and more empowered future.

CHAPTER 3 STEP 3

Living with my abuser

Coping with emotionally immature, toxic, and abusive parents.

Navigating Relationships

For a survivor of abuse, navigating relationships with emotionally immature, toxic, or abusive parents can be a susceptible and complex matter. The impact of past abuse can significantly influence how one manages present relationships, especially with parents who still exhibit these behaviours, as interacting with them can hinder the healing process from past abuse as it can trigger emotional distress, anxiety, or re-traumatisation.

For all these reasons, it is essential to have a strategy in place if one is to continue to have a relationship with these family members. Prioritising your mental and emotional well-being is crucial. If maintaining contact or dealing with these parents compromises your stability or causes distress, it might be necessary to reevaluate the level of engagement. While challenging, navigating these relationships can offer an opportunity to reinforce personal boundaries and assertiveness. Learning to set limits and protect yourself is a crucial skill for survivors of abuse.

Factors to Consider: Your mental health and stability should be the priority. If interacting with these parents negatively impacts your well-being, reconsider the level of engagement. You will need a strong support network, whether friends, a therapist, or support groups, which will be pivotal in providing guidance and emotional reinforcement.

However, suppose there's any risk to your physical or mental safety. In that case, it might be necessary to limit or cut off contact with them.

Seeking professional guidance: consulting with a therapist or counsellor can provide specific strategies to manage interactions and process the emotions associated with these relationships. Support groups or organisations specialising in assisting abuse survivors can offer guidance and a safe space to share experiences.

The decision to navigate relationships with emotionally immature or abusive parents is highly personal and complex. Key aspects are prioritising your well-being and mental health, setting boundaries, and seeking support. Your emotional and physical safety and peace of mind should guide your decisions regarding these relationships.

Developing communication skills: Developing strong communication skills is pivotal when dealing with an abusive parent. While challenging, effective communication can mitigate the severity of conflicts and create opportunities for setting boundaries, expressing concerns, and fostering a more stable relationship.

Communication skills are crucial because they empower us to establish and assert healthy boundaries. Clearly articulating what behaviour is acceptable or unacceptable can help minimise the impact of the abuse.

Effective communication allows you to express your needs and concerns non-confrontationally; this might involve using "I" statements to convey feelings and requests without triggering hostility. Clear and effective communication helps define and understand each other's expectations; this reduces misunderstandings and potential triggers for abusive behaviour .

De-escalating conflict: communication skills are essential for diffusing or de-escalating conflicts. Techniques such as active listening, empathy, and strategic language can help you navigate tense situations more smoothly. Encouraging open and empathetic communication might foster compassion in the other person over time. However challenging, better communication could prompt a better understanding of your perspective.

Developing communication skills can also aid in seeking external help. Communicating your situation clearly to friends, therapists, or authorities is crucial for getting the support you need.

Practical communication skills will also improve self-advocacy, enabling you to stand up for yourself without aggravating or provoking further abuse. It will also allow you to maintain control in emotionally charged situations; learning to choose these responses strategically will help to minimise the impact of abusive behaviour and reduce the likelihood of exacerbating the problem. All of these are vital to safeguarding your mental, physical, and emotional well-being.

Developing communication skills when dealing with an abusive parent is an ongoing process that involves patience, practice, and a willingness to adapt. While it might not completely change the dynamics of the relationship, it equips you with tools to navigate better and cope with the challenges presented by an abusive parent. However, it's essential to remember that in situations of severe abuse, prioritising your safety and well-being might necessitate seeking external help or establishing distance from the abusive behaviour.

How past experiences affect adult relationships.

Understanding how past experiences affect our adult relationships is fundamental and critical to healing and personal growth. After studying all these behaviour patterns in the previous chapter, we should be in a great position to recognise these in the people around us, start making sense of many situations we have gone through, and answer many of the questions we have had for years.

It is essential to consider the following to heal from these experiences and gain control of our lives.

Trigger awareness: Recognising how past abuse can trigger certain emotions, reactions, or behaviours in adult relationships is the first step to managing them effectively. By identifying these triggers, we can respond more consciously and choose healthier answers. Our main objective is ***Breaking Harmful Patterns***: as we know, we can unconsciously replicate unhealthy relationship patterns learned in childhood, so understanding the source of these patterns is essential for breaking the cycle and establishing healthier dynamics in adult relationships.

Past abuse can erode trust and hinder effective relationship communication. Acknowledging this impact will allow us to work on rebuilding trust and developing open, honest, and constructive communication skills with our loved ones and all the people around us. However, ***Setting Healthy Boundaries*** will be essential for establishing healthy relationships with them.

Regarding ***Emotional Intimacy and Vulnerability***, our past experiences can create barriers. As survivors, we can work toward developing deeper emotional connections in our adult relationships by recognising these. Understanding the origins of low self-esteem and a negative self-image will challenge us and rebuild our self-worth, which is crucial for healthy relationships.

Healing Past Trauma: As survivors of abuse, we may carry unresolved trauma into our adult relationships. Acknowledging this trauma is the first step toward seeking the necessary healing and support to address it. Doing this will empower us to make conscious choices in relationships. We can choose partners who respect our boundaries, values, and well-being.

Recognising the effects of past abuse underscores the importance of ***self-care and self-compassion***. We can prioritise our well-being and healing by positively influencing our relationships. Understanding the link between past abuse and adult relationship challenges will motivate us to seek professional help or join support groups. All of these resources offer guidance, validation, and strategies for healing.

Rebuilding relationships

It is vital to understand that, depending on our circumstances, we could face very different scenarios.

In the case of dealing with ***emotionally immature parents*** from a childhood of emotional neglect, it is possible to build a good relationship by working with them to become more aware of their emotions and maturing them. I f they wish they could overcome these and become more present within their relationships we will be able to rebuild relationships and live in harmony with them.

On the contrary, when it comes to more toxic personality traits like ***narcissism or sociopath***, if members of your family or your close circle have these personality disorders, it is essential to recognise and acknowledge these, as in that case, we will have to accept or come to terms with the reality that these people may never change. First and foremost, they don't think anything is wrong with them; we have to change to suit them. Learning to manage our relationship with them will be crucial as we do not want to end up being manipulated and hurt by them.

I understand that this may be difficult to accept, as many of these are people we care about very much, but that is the reality. These personality traits have deep and complicated roots that can only be treated by professionals, that is, if they recognise there is an issue and that they need to look for help to overcome it.

Unfortunately, most of the time, they are convinced that everything is fine with them and that the rest of us have the problem. Therefore, there is little hope they will change. If we love them, we are the ones that have to change around them, to be in control and not allow them to manipulate us or hurt us. We cannot expect to change them with our love or the sacrifice we will make for them.

You may think, *"But is my family, my mum, my brother, my sister?"* For this very reason, you must not allow them to carry on hurting you, abuse you, or exploit you. You may think that because you love them, you will take it upon yourself to try to fix them, but you must accept that this will never happen. Instead, you could end up wrapped up in their issues, which could affect you psychologically and, consequently, physically. (It has been known that many chronic illnesses have their roots in psychological traumas). Instead, it is crucial to learn how to deal with them (that is if you choose to continue a relationship with them). Sometimes, there may be no choice but to cut all relations with these individuals, whoever they may be.

The Effect of Emotionally Immature, Abusive and Toxic Parents on the Adult Children.

What we live through in childhood inevitably affects our lives as adults, our behaviour, how we interact with the people around us, and, more importantly, what kind of parents we become.

As I have mentioned, one of the main reasons I decided to write this book was when I realised that I was starting to behave like my Mother. Consciously, my main objective was to build a good relationship with my children to be a mum they knew they could talk to. Instead, I was having some reactions that were coming out entirely unconsciously, responses that I could not control, and ideas that conflicted with me essentially but also questioned if they were correct. I hated the relationship I had with my Mother; I had moved thousands of miles away from her as I just wanted to put as much distance as possible between us. She constantly made me feel like a failure as if I was always doing everything wrong. Coming away was like admitting I would never be good enough for her, and being as far away as possible was the only way I could endure that.

Becoming a mum has challenged those issues very much. When I had my daughter, I was determined to do the best job possible to be a good mum, but I needed help. I had a tremendous conflict with some of my ideas about being a parent. I was raised in a dictatorial household and hated it, but I knew nothing different.

When I started having some reactions that I could not explain and that made me feel physically sick, I realised I had to do something. I had to understand where my responses were coming from; the parenthood ideas and behaviours I was so against were manifesting in me, and I had no control over them.

Only then did I realise that I had been walking around with a significant burden, a hugely painful and empty space inside me that, somehow, I was going to have to face. I would have to do some acknowledgement and reprogramming to be the mum I so desperately wanted to become.

At this point, understanding how past experiences affect adult relationships was the key to breaking the cycle. We can break free from the limitations of our past and build healthier, more fulfilling relationships based on mutual respect, and for this, gaining insight into the impact of past abuse on adult relationships was vital. It allowed me to confront the past, make conscious choices, seek healing and support, and build healthier and more satisfying connections as a mum and with others.

This self-awareness is a powerful tool for breaking free from the chains of abuse and forging a brighter future filled with love, trust, and meaningful relationships with everybody around us. Unresolved Issues from the past can sometimes act as a trigger of behaviour or reactions we do not recognise.

Sometimes, we may find ourselves in uncomfortable situations; this could be because it reminds us of an experience we have gone through; these situations may cause a reaction that we are not expecting, which could be unpleasant for us and the people around us. Taking a moment to acknowledge what has happened, analyse it, and understand where this may have come from may be an excellent first step. At this point, we must recognise that how we feel may not have anything to do with the present situation or person we are dealing with but with the internal unresolved issue we may have. For the sake of our relationships, we have to look at that reaction, acknowledge it, and trace it back to its origins. This exercise will allow us to understand and recognise the response; this small step will help us gain control of those reactions and help us express ourselves healthily, allowing us to build healthier relationships with the people around us, especially those we love.

Doing this will allow us to recognise situations that may trigger our reactions and be in a better position to control them and not be affected by them any longer.

How do we cope with being a child of an emotionally immature, toxic, or abusive parent, and how can this shape our adult relationships?

Having emotionally immature, toxic, or abusive parents is traumatic for a child. We often see children developing coping mechanisms to survive their experiences in these cases. Psychologist Lindsay C. Gibson, the author of *Adult Children of Emotionally Immature Parents,* talks about *Healing Fantasies* and *Role-Self* as common coping mechanisms for children living in challenging family/home environments. Let us analyse these mechanisms in more depth below.

Healing fantasies: When I was young, my mother often called me a dreamer because I was always "daydreaming." I would take every opportunity to imagine I had caring and never-angry parents. Creating a healing fantasy helped me cope with my reality.

Psychologist Lindsay C. Gibson talks about ***Role-Self;*** this behaviour usually happens when the child believes they must become someone else to be noticed or even accepted by their parent. They end up making this colossal character their parents like and never showing themself for who they are. My parent always expected a lot from me; they always struggled financially and somehow rested all their hopes on me to help them. They idealised me so much that they saw me as a superhero who would solve all their issues. My father used to call me my Wonder Woman!! Looking back on it, I can see they were desperate for someone to curtail their responsibility, problems, and issues.

I did everything I could to please them to earn and secure my place within my family. My parents' goals and aspirations and family rules squashed my ***true self.*** But the issue was that I am not or was not a superhero; I was becoming a young adult and had my dreams and aspirations. My true self was bubbling up to the surface, and I could not continue to work hard for what they wanted as I had my dreams and goals to make a reality.

Unfortunately, these coping mechanisms would very often be carried to adulthood, bringing a different set of challenges to our adult relationships, as we may walk into a relationship hoping or even expecting this to provide us with what we did not get from our family growing up and get very disappointed if we don't. Sometimes, we do everything our partner wants, hoping that we will get from them the love and attention we deserve in return, only to find ourselves wholly disappointed when things don't work out the way we hope; this is why it is essential to become aware of our childhood personal experiences and recognise any psychological traumas we may have so we can work on overcoming these to live a more full-felt adult life.

An adult child of an abusive parent. How does it feel?

*"Christmas was approaching, and Mother had asked me to buy an expensive gift for my younger sister (the golden child); I did not have the money to do this because I had already spent my Christmas bonus buying presents for the whole family and dressing all my three younger brothers and sisters in new shoes and clothes for the festivities. My Mother was unhappy; she told me she was disappointed in me **for not fulfilling her wish,** and she decided to*

punish me by treating me with total indifference for the duration of the holiday and several weeks afterwards".

These kinds of scenarios were prevalent and happened very often on a smaller or larger scale; in some cases, I remember them as if they happened yesterday, but apart from the emotional pain of not being able to please my Mother, to make her happy (as that is what I was there for, to please her) despite all my effort, the psychological scars of her behaviour and the way she treated me were very damaging and left me with many psychological traumas that I am still working to overcome today.

Self-doubt, Anxiety, and Lack of Confidence are just some of the issues we can be left to deal with when we come from a home with *emotionally immature, toxic, and abusive parents.*

I remember very well noticing one of the first signs of my trauma when I could not speak up or express myself in difficult situations, and I would just burst into tears without speaking a word. I did not know who I was, and I did not know what to believe in. When I think about that time, I feel like I had a massive void and could not explain it.

I believe that is the worst thing about this legacy of abuse: the level of anxiety and insecurity that we are left to deal with daily. The pain and suffering that these feelings of insecurity and anxiety have put me through have jeopardised my professional life, my family, my marriage, and even my own life at points, and in some ways, I am still battling with today as I have to make a conscious effort to keep myself positive and handling the negatives situations and not let the anxiety and insecurity take over.

Since I realised that my parents had abused me physically, physiologically, and financially for many years, many of those voids I had in my life have found an explanation. I could then understand some of these feelings.

These experiences could cause many personality issues as we grow up, as we could become people-pleasers, always working to do/be what other people want us to do/be, never fully owning our true selves, and never reaching our full potential; this will bring more issues in the future as we get frustrated for not being able to realise our true selves.

It is essential to be conscious of our experiences and what we lived through, acknowledge it, and work through it to overcome it, as well as become aware of the emotional immaturity and toxicity of our parents, accepting that they most probably will never change and taking control of our relationship with them is fundamental and the only way not to get hurt.

Rebuilding trust and forming new bonds after such experiences can be incredibly challenging but sometimes possible with time, patience, and self-care.

Stay in touch or cut the links?

There are only two paths when taking action and dealing with our emotionally immature, abusive, toxic relatives.

In most cases, these are our closest relatives: parents, brothers, or sisters, and for this reason, it is complicated to imagine our life without them. So it is understandable we want to continue to have a relationship with these people.

Suppose this is the case, and we decide to continue in a relationship with them. In that case, this must be done by taking certain precautions, so we don't allow them to continue manipulating, suppressing, or hurting us.

We can only achieve this by taking control and establishing clear boundaries in our relationship with them. Now, we must never forget that they will not ever change and that we are the ones who need to change the way we deal with them. We must not forget that we can only control how we act around them, which we must work on continuously.

We often secretly hope that things will be different one day or that we can help them change because they are our parents, and we love them. In my own experience, I hoped that would be the case. I thought that after 15 years of being away from them, they would have been thrilled and supportive of their daughter and her family coming back to live in the country, only to find that all the old habits were not just still there but were ever more toxic as they now had deeper roots.

So establishing boundary rules is the only way to maintain control and protect ourselves if we stay in these relationships; it is imperative to keep this in mind the whole time.

However, be aware that they may respond to your boundaries differently than you would like them to; as I mentioned, you can only control how you behave around them and your response to their behaviour. What you are prepared to tolerate and when you will stop them from abusing, controlling, or exploiting you is totally in your hands.

Again, it is fundamental to remember that you are not doing this to help them realise what they are doing is wrong, change their behaviour or educate them. If you get that outcome, it will be fantastic, but that rarely happens. They cannot and will not recognise these as they believe there is nothing wrong with their behaviour. I hoped for many years for them to see the hurt they were causing me, only to find myself back at square one with a new wound to try to heal and more trauma to overcome. We must accept this and come to terms with it, so setting obvious boundaries is the only way to stay in these relationships.

Let's talk about setting boundaries in more detail.

Setting and maintaining boundaries is of paramount importance when recovering from abuse. As survivors of abuse, it's crucial to emphasise the significance of establishing healthy boundaries as part of our healing journey and recovery process. Some key reasons for this are:

Self-Protection: Boundaries serve as a protective shield; they help us establish limits to prevent further harm or abuse. They act as a safeguard against invasive or harmful behaviours from others.

Reclaiming Personal Power: we often lose personal power and control during this struggle. Setting boundaries empowers us to regain a sense of agency over our lives and decisions, it reinforces the idea that we have the right to determine what is acceptable and what is not in our lives.

Emotional Well-Being: Boundaries protect emotional well-being. They allow us to prioritise our mental and emotional health, ensuring we are not overwhelmed or manipulated by others' emotions or actions.

Healthy Relationships: Healthy boundaries are the foundation; they enable individuals to engage in relationships characterised by mutual respect, understanding, and consideration for each other's needs and limits.

Reduction of Re-Victimisation: Without clear boundaries, we may be at risk of entering into or remaining in abusive relationships. Setting limits helps identify and avoid potentially harmful situations.

Communication Skills: Establishing boundaries requires effective communication. It is essential to promote the development of assertive communication skills, which are valuable in all areas of life.

Increased Self-Esteem: Respecting and enforcing boundaries sends the powerful message that we deserve respect and consideration; this will contribute to an improved self-image and higher self-esteem.

Building Trust: Healthy boundaries contribute to the development of trust in relationships. We can trust ourselves and others more fully if our limits are consistently respected.

Personal Growth: Establishing and maintaining boundaries is vital to personal growth and self-discovery. It involves self-awareness and self-advocacy, which are essential for recovery.

Conflict Resolution: Boundaries can aid in conflict resolution by providing a framework for addressing disagreements and finding compromises that respect everyone's needs. *Positive Role Modelling:* As we learn to set boundaries, we become positive role models for others, including our children, friends, and family members.

It's important to note that setting boundaries can be challenging, especially for survivors of abuse who may have been conditioned to ignore their own needs and prioritise the needs of others. As a survivor of abuse, navigating this process of validation and practical strategies for boundary-setting is essential and the key to succeeding in establishing healthy relationships with our loved ones. We can start small and gradually expand our boundaries as we become more comfortable and confident in asserting our needs and limits.

Understand and communicate your boundaries.

What is important to you, what are your limits, what are you willing to accept, and what are you not? It is your right to be respected and to refuse any situation where you are bullied or bombarded with negativity and abuse. It is natural and part of our instinct as humans to protect ourselves. We are not bad for asking not to be bullied or abused; we practice self-care. These mechanisms could help our relatives understand and recognise when they are going too far, and we are unwilling to tolerate their behaviour any longer.

Communicating your boundaries: Make sure you clearly and consistently communicate these boundaries. Keeping control of your emotions whilst doing this will be fundamental. Suppose you break down emotionally during the conversation. In that case, you will lose all control of the situation, and they will not take you seriously. Assertiveness and strength in these situations are crucial to success. We must remember that we are doing this for their good, our sanity and well-being, and our relationship if we are to have one with them.

Record what is happening. Writing down what is happening and how you reacted to the situation would be very productive; this will help you to analyse what had happened with a cool head at a later date and recognise what you could have done differently to avoid confrontation and get your point across better next time. Writing is also a potent healing tool and excellent for our mental health.

Following your intentions: You must stay assertive and firm with the boundaries you have set out, which may be disrespected and violated several times before the person realises you are serious about this. It would help if you kept consistency in doing this, as whatever terrain you lose in these fights will take twice the effort to regain. You may have to follow up with *consequences*; some people can only understand the direct reactions to their actions.

Cutting the cord: If, after all these, they still disrespect you and your space, it may be time to start practising detachment in a caring but firm way.

Some ways to do this may be removing yourself physically from an uncomfortable situation that involves them, and stopping yourself from advising when it was not requested. Avoid engaging in conversations that could be unproductive and lead to an argument. Declining invitations to spend too much time with them and being assertive and firm when dealing with them in any circumstances.

However, despite all these, there may be cases where cutting relations is the only solution. I grew up thinking that family is all and that we would always be there for each other, so the thought of cutting all relations with my family was unthinkable. Only when I realised that the most precious thing to me, my own family, was in jeopardy I did acknowledge that I had no alternative, but removing myself and my family was the only alternative.

In summary, setting boundaries is a crucial component of healing from abuse. It empowers us to stand up for ourselves, protects our well-being, and fosters healthy relationships. Reclaiming our sense of self-worth and building a life that is defined by safety, respect, and empowerment.

CHAPTER 4 STEP 4

Cutting the links

As we know, cutting ties with toxic family members is a complex and emotionally challenging decision that individuals may make for various psychological, emotional, and sometimes financial reasons. It's important to note that this decision is highly personal and context dependent. Only some people will have to choose to do so, depending on the circumstances. Still, some people are sometimes left with no alternative other than stopping contact with these family members. Bellow, I would like to talk about some psychological factors that may contribute to the decision to cut ties with our toxic family members so we can understand these better.

Self-Preservation: One of the primary reasons people distance themselves from toxic family members is to protect their own mental and emotional well-being. Toxic individuals can be emotionally abusive, manipulative, and draining, causing significant distress and harm to their family members. Over time, the individual may realise that maintaining the relationship is detrimental to their mental health and self-esteem. Boundary Setting or cutting ties with toxic family members can be seen as establishing healthy boundaries. Some individuals may have grown up in environments where boundaries were not respected, and they may decide to distance themselves as a way of asserting their autonomy and self-worth.

Emotional Healing: Ending a relationship with a toxic family member can be a step toward emotional healing and personal growth. It allows individuals to focus on their emotional well-being and seek therapy or support to address the emotional scars and traumas they may have experienced in the toxic relationship.

Role Modelling: For individuals who are parents themselves, cutting ties with a toxic family member can be a way to set a positive example for their children. They may not want their children to witness or internalise unhealthy patterns of behaviour, and they choose to break the cycle by distancing themselves from toxic influences.

Respect for Ourselves: Self-respect is a crucial psychological factor in this decision. People may come to a point where they recognise that maintaining a relationship with a toxic family member is inconsistent with their values and self-respect. They may prioritise their dignity and well-being over maintaining a dysfunctional connection.

Mental Health: Chronic exposure to toxic family members can contribute to mental health issues such as anxiety, depression, and low self-esteem. Cutting ties may be a strategy for improving one's mental health and seeking professional help to address the psychological consequences of the toxic relationship.

Empowerment: Deciding to cut ties with a toxic family member can be empowering. It represents a choice to take control of one's life and not be held hostage by unhealthy relationships. This empowerment can boost an individual's self-esteem and overall psychological well-being.

It's important to note that deciding to cut ties with a family member is not easy, and it can come with emotional challenges and feelings of guilt or grief. Many individuals may choose therapy or support from friends and other loved ones during this process. Additionally, not all situations may warrant cutting ties, and some individuals may opt for strategies like limited contact or setting clear boundaries instead. Ultimately, the decision should be guided by the best interest of the individual's psychological, emotional, and physical health.

I am the oldest daughter of 5 children. My parents also came from large families, so as I have mentioned before, I grew up thinking that family is everything and that they will always be there for each other. Despite all the traumatic issues that went on behind closed doors, the possibility of cutting all relations with my family never crossed my mind. I did have many tough times with them. Things did worsen with the years and with my parents getting older, especially my mother, but never did I think I was going to spend so much time not speaking to them or having no relationship with them.

I know that this may be a difficult thing to understand for many people, especially for people in a culture where parents are seen as god-like figures who have to be worshipped, obeyed, and adored by their children. The issue is that they are not gods; they are just humans full of flaws and errors like any other humans. Unfortunately, they have had so much power over their children's lives for so many years; they could make that child the happiest and most successful individual as well as the most traumatised and unhappy human they can be, causing terrible damage to their children's psychological, mental and physical health and integrity, rooting deep trauma that could very often materialise in physical illness which in some cases could be very dangerous as it could jeopardise their health in many ways.

There is also all the noise around us, people's opinions that sometimes push us to comply with and accept things that we disagree with and are fundamentally against. These experiences send a profound negative message to our subconscious, telling us that what they think or want from us is more important than what we believe or want for ourselves. Imagine being constantly abused by your parents and being told by everyone else around you that you must find a way to have a better relationship with them, completely ignoring what is happening to you and the hurt that this may be causing you. The messages these behaviours, actions, or comments send to our subconscious are tremendously powerful and negative simultaneously, *"They are the ones that matter"* and *"Your feelings are not valid"*. These messages have the power to crush that child/person, making them believe it is okay to be treated like that or, even worse, that they deserve to be treated in that way.

I remember so many fights I had with my mother, which most of the time would end up in physical aggression on her part towards me, only to have friends and family members telling me I should put more effort into finding a way to get on with my mother. The message was that over everything, she was my mother, and that was more important than the physical and psychological abuse I was systematically subjected to. That was the constant message I was repeatedly told: ***"But it is your mum"*** or ***"You only have one mother."***

Unfortunately, this kept happening until not long ago; even though I had come away from them and put physical distance between us, my mother still had a massive influence on me. I was still psychologically and financially exploited by her.

Only when I realised that their ill behaviour was starting to affect my own family, my children and my marriage did I come to terms with the reality that nothing was ever going to change, no matter how much effort I put into it and how much I tried, there was nothing that I could do to satisfy them or solve their issues.

The day my mother told me that she was more important than my children and that I should always prioritise her was a massive turning point. I finally realised that I needed to take action. I needed to do something; unfortunately, the only thing left was to cut all links with them. It was clear that my children came before anything, that they needed me more than anyone, and that I wanted to be there for them no matter what; this was a challenging time in my life, and it hurt to realise and accept that unless I could benefit them, they had no interest in me, especially my mother. Unless I did precisely as she wanted, she was prepared to punish me, or I would even say ruin me.

As I was growing up, I was always told by my mother that I was problematic, challenging to live with, and a bad daughter in general. She always treated me like the black sheep of the family and used to say it all the time again and again to me, to the rest of the family, and even to my friends and I believed it.

Nevertheless, something significant happened then, making me question the whole thing. I realised that I was horrible when I did not do what my parents wanted; this made me suspect that maybe the problem was not in me. It seemed like someone turned the switch on for me, and I could suddenly see. It was like an incredible wake-up call, and I was not such a terrible person as she tried to make me believe my whole life. On the contrary, I was an excellent first older daughter; I helped and supported my parents, looked after my younger brothers and sisters, and gave them everything I could.

However, I also realised at that point that no matter what I did, it was never going to be enough for my mother; I could finally see that the only thing she cared about was herself and how I was going to cater to her, how I could be beneficial to her and what she cared about. My mother was prepared to lie and fall accused to coerce me to do what she wanted; she was dangerous. My happiness or well-being and my family were not in her interest.

That period was one of the darkest times in my life; for the first time, I learned what it felt like to be heartbroken. I felt abandoned by them, an orphan at the same time. I could not explain the pain I felt as I realised, I was betrayed, stubbed, and turned back on by my own family. Then, it felt like I was walking through a very dark and cold tunnel that I could not see the end of.

However, in early 2020, I got diagnosed with an autoimmune condition; this was another massive turning point in my life and, again, an enormous wake-up call. All these very traumatic experiences have affected my health. I have to take responsibility and understand what happened and what I could do to help myself get to good health again for my own sake, mental, psychological, and physical health, for my children and my family.

Psychological Trauma and Autoimmune Disease

Psychological trauma and autoimmune diseases are two complex and multifaceted areas of study within the fields of psychology and medicine. While they may seem unrelated on the surface, emerging research has shown that there is a significant relationship between psychological trauma and the development and exacerbation of autoimmune diseases. In this book section, I would like to explore the intricate interplay between these two phenomena, considering the biological, psychological, and social factors contributing to their connection. Look into the mechanisms through which trauma may trigger or exacerbate autoimmune diseases, the role of stress and the immune system, and the implications for clinical practice and future research.

The book *What Happened to You? Oprah Winfrey and Dr. Bruce Perry* talk about how all our childhood experiences are very closely linked to our behaviour as adults and the physical damage that psychological trauma can cause in our lives. There have also been studies where up to 80% of adults taking part have reported extreme levels of emotional and psychological stress immediately before they were diagnosed with autoimmune diseases. In these situations, we can see abnormal levels of stress hormones leading to dysregulation of the immune system, which could lead to auto-destruction of the body's tissues.

With this, researchers have demonstrated that there is a distinctive connection between mind and body, and studies continue to validate this, paying particular attention to the relationship between childhood trauma and the inflammatory and autoimmune response.

However, *The long-term health effects* on individuals who have suffered *Adverse Childhood Experiences or Stressful Events in Adulthood* are not limited to autoimmune diseases. People who have been exposed to these experiences are more prone to mental illnesses, substance abuse, and other health issues such as heart attack, which shows that human physical, mental, psychological, spiritual, and social health are all very closely linked.

Let's take a look at these with more attention.

Psychological trauma encompasses a range of adverse experiences, such as physical, emotional, or sexual abuse, as well as exposure to natural disasters or war combat, which can have lasting psychological and physiological effects on individuals.

Autoimmune diseases are a group of disorders characterised by the immune system's abnormal response to extreme stress, leading it to attack the body's tissues and organs. These conditions, including Rheumatoid Arthritis, Lupus, Multiple Sclerosis, and Hashimoto's Thyroiditis, affect millions of individuals worldwide. Recent research has shown a compelling connection between psychological trauma and the development or exacerbation of autoimmune diseases; here are various dimensions of this relationship.

Mechanisms Underlying this Relationship.

Dysregulation of the Immune System: Psychological trauma can lead to chronic stress, activating the body's stress response system and resulting in the release of stress hormones like cortisol. Prolonged stress can dysregulate the immune system, making it more prone to inflammation and autoimmune responses. Chronic stress may lead to the overproduction of pro-inflammatory cytokines, which can contribute to the onset and progression of autoimmune diseases.

Epigenetic Changes: Epigenetic modifications are changes to the DNA molecule or associated proteins that can affect gene expression without altering the underlying DNA sequence. These modifications are crucial in regulating gene activity. They are essential for various biological processes, including development, differentiation, and response to environmental cues. Emerging research suggests that traumatic experiences can lead to epigenetic modifications, altering gene expression patterns in ways that increase susceptibility to autoimmune diseases. These changes may affect immune system functioning and promote autoimmune responses.

Psychological Factors: Psychological trauma can have long-lasting psychological effects, including depression, anxiety, and post-traumatic stress disorder (PTSD). These psychological conditions are known to have immune system implications, and individuals with autoimmune diseases often experience symptom exacerbation during periods of high psychological distress.

Childhood Trauma has been strongly linked to the development of autoimmune diseases later in life. Adverse childhood experiences (ACEs), such as abuse, neglect, or household dysfunction, can have lasting effects on stress responses and immune function. These early-life traumas may set the stage for autoimmune susceptibility.

Social and Environmental Factors: The social determinants of health play a significant role in the relationship between trauma and autoimmune diseases. Individuals with lower socioeconomic status may face more traumatic experiences and have less access to healthcare, exacerbating their risk for autoimmune diseases. Moreover, the lack of social support and coping resources can contribute to both trauma and autoimmune disease risk.

Implications for Clinical Practice and Research

An integrated care approach should be aware of the potential link between psychological trauma and autoimmune diseases. Integrated care that addresses both psychological well-being and physical health is crucial for effectively managing these conditions for trauma survivors, and providing early interventions, such as trauma-focused therapy, may mitigate the long-term impact of trauma on autoimmune disease development.

Further research is needed to understand the specific mechanisms and pathways connecting trauma and autoimmune diseases. Longitudinal studies, epigenetic research, and clinical trials exploring the effects of trauma-focused interventions on autoimmune disease outcomes are essential for advancing our knowledge.

However, a holistic approach to treating autoimmune diseases and other health conditions is essential. Ideally, we pay attention to all aspects of our lives by taking responsibility and doing what we must to look after ourselves by optimising our diet, looking after our microbiome, and balancing our hormones. Also, considering all the mental health aspects, like addressing anxiety, depression, and trauma and learning coping mechanisms to deal with these, is massively helpful.

Connecting with people with similar stories has been hugely beneficial for me, as sharing common ground with them allowed me and the other person to work through some issues and gradually overcome them or cope with them better.

In a research done by Dr Izabella Wentz, after being diagnosed with Hashimoto's Thyroiditis, she talks about a lifestyle change and an approach combining integrative and functional medicines.

Integrative medicine is an approach to healthcare that combines conventional Western medicine with complementary and alternative therapies, aiming to address not only the physical aspects of a patient's health but also their emotional, social, and spiritual well-being. This approach is rooted in a holistic view of health, where the patient is seen as a whole person, and the goal is to achieve a balanced state of well-being rather than merely treating specific diseases or symptoms.

Integrative medicine's key features include the ***Holistic Approach:*** Integrative medicine practitioners consider the physical, mental, emotional, social, and spiritual aspects of a patient's health. They believe these elements are interconnected and that addressing them can improve overall well-being.

Combination of Therapies: Integrative medicine combines evidence-based conventional medical treatments with complementary and alternative therapies, such as acupuncture, herbal medicine, mind-body practices (e.g., yoga, meditation), nutritional counselling, and more. The selection of treatments is tailored to the individual patient's needs and preferences.

Patient-Centred Care: Patients are actively involved in the decision-making process regarding their healthcare. The approach emphasises patient education, empowerment, and the development of a therapeutic partnership between the patient and the healthcare provider. **Prevention and Lifestyle:** Integrative medicine often emphasises preventive strategies and healthy lifestyle choices, recognising the significance of diet, exercise, stress management, and other factors in promoting health and preventing disease.

Integrative medicine seeks to integrate *Evidence-based practices* from both conventional and complementary therapies; this includes ongoing research to evaluate the safety and effectiveness of various treatments. *Collaboration and Team-Based Care:* Integrative medicine often involves collaboration between healthcare providers, including medical doctors, naturopathic physicians, chiropractors, acupuncturists, nutritionists, and mental health professionals. These healthcare professionals work together to provide a comprehensive and coordinated approach to patient care.

It's important to note that while integrative medicine aims to incorporate the best of both conventional and complementary therapies, it also emphasises evidence-based practices. Not all complementary and alternative therapies are supported by scientific evidence, and their use may vary based on individual patient needs and preferences. It's essential to approach integrative medicine with a critical and evidence-based mindset, examining the scientific basis for various treatments and their potential benefits and risks. Research in this field can contribute to a better understanding of the efficacy and safety of integrative approaches and help inform clinical practice and patient care.

Functional medicine is an approach to healthcare that focuses on understanding and addressing the underlying root causes of illness and dysfunction rather than merely treating the symptoms. It is a patient-centred, systems-based approach that explores the interconnectedness of various bodily systems and the influence of lifestyle, genetics, and the environment on an individual's health. It is essential to recognise that functional medicine is an evolving field combining conventional medicine elements with a more holistic and personalised approach.

Key characteristics and principles of functional medicine include *systems biology,* which views the body as an interconnected web of systems rather than a collection of isolated parts. Practitioners consider how various methods—such as the digestive, hormonal, immune, and neurological systems- interact and influence one another in health and disease.

Personalised Care: The approach is highly individualised, with healthcare providers seeking to understand each patient's unique genetic, biochemical, and environmental factors; this enables the development of personalised treatment plans tailored to the specific needs and circumstances of the patient. *Root Cause Analysis:* Functional medicine practitioners aim to identify and address the underlying causes of a patient's health issues, such as chronic inflammation, imbalances in nutrition, toxins, infections, and lifestyle factors. By addressing these root causes, they aim to support the body's inherent ability to heal.

Like integrative medicine, functional medicine strongly emphasises preventive strategies and lifestyle interventions; this includes dietary changes, exercise, stress management, and other factors promoting health and well-being. Functional medicine often involves a collaborative and multidisciplinary approach, with practitioners from different healthcare disciplines working together to address all aspects of a patient's health; this may include medical doctors, nutritionists, naturopathic physicians, and other specialists.

Scientific Basis: While functional medicine considers a wide range of diagnostic and therapeutic options, it strives to be evidence-based; this means practitioners should use scientific research and clinical evidence to support their diagnostic and treatment decisions.

Researchers are crucial in contributing to functional medicine's scientific knowledge and evidence base; they are involved in studies to evaluate the effectiveness and safety of various functional medicine interventions, exploring the mechanisms underlying chronic diseases, and investigating the impact of genetic factors on health outcomes.

Functional medicine is an evolving field that has gained attention for its patient-centred and holistic approach. It can be valuable to conventional medical practices, particularly for chronic and complex health conditions. However, it's essential to maintain a critical and evidence-based approach to ensure that the principles and interventions of functional medicine are rigorously tested and validated through research.

In conclusion, the relationship between psychological trauma and autoimmune diseases is a multifaceted and evolving field of study. While the mechanisms underlying this connection are not yet fully understood, evidence suggests that trauma can dysregulate the immune system, trigger epigenetic changes, and exacerbate autoimmune responses. Recognising this relationship is crucial for clinicians, as it informs a more holistic approach to patient care. Further research will continue to shed light on the intricate interplay between trauma and autoimmune diseases, offering hope for improved prevention and treatment strategies for all these conditions.

CHAPTER 5 STEP 5

Forgiveness is a form of healing.

"Stop hoping for a better past." Dr Fred Luskin

Forgiveness and Closure.

Writing this book has been both challenging and liberating at the same time, as it has required me to acknowledge, learn, recognise, and understand situations and behaviours to grow and overcome internal conflicts and traumas. However, without any doubt, I can say that this chapter is probably the most important in the whole process as I believe it holds the key to the main objective of the entire book, which is overcoming the legacy left by the relationship with my Emotionally Immature, Toxic and Abusive Parents and becoming genuinely free of guilt and happy again.

Forgiveness is a complex and multifaceted psychological process that holds the power to heal emotional wounds, repair relationships, and promote overall well-being. It is a fundamental human experience that transcends cultural, religious, and social boundaries. It is a process through which individuals let go of resentment, anger, and the desire for revenge towards those who have wronged them.

At this point, it's important to note that forgiveness is a very personal process, and it could be a very challenging and painful request for someone who has been a victim of abuse and experienced trauma. Below, I would like to emphasise what forgiveness is not.

1- It Does Not mean condoning or excusing the wrong that was done; we do not have to accept wrong, hurtful, and offensive behaviour.

2- It does not mean that you have to erase the memory of the wrongdoing; these memories are often harrowing, so we are better at acknowledging them instead of trying to erase them; this will help the healing process.

3- Pretend it never happened; this could be hazardous, as the damage these wrongdoings or behaviours may have caused us could bring other more complicated psychological and physical issues. Honouring these feelings and permitting ourselves to experience them entirely is essential.

4- You do not have to absolve the perpetrators; we do not have to declare them free from guilt or obligation. Life is accurate in accounting for our actions and whatever bills we may have to pay.

5- You do not have to let them off the hook; we do not have to allow them to escape from the situation or avoid taking responsibility for their actions.

6- Although conciliation could be an outcome for some people, it is only for some. Forgiving does not always mean reconciling with the person who had caused us hurt; we may even decide not to have any relationship with them again.

Instead, forgiveness is about *Letting Go of Negative Emotions and feelings towards someone*. In this process, we release negative emotions such as anger, resentment, and hatred that arise when someone has wronged us. It is a conscious choice to free ourselves from the emotional burden these feelings can create.

It involves a conscious decision to let go of the desire for revenge, which can lead to emotional and physical healing and bring peace to our lives. However, forgiveness is not always easy and may require time and effort, especially in significant harm or betrayal cases. Still, it is essential to understand how good it can be for ourselves to forgive.

By letting go of these emotions, we allow ourselves to heal and move forward, and this is the forgiveness that I would like to focus on. I want to explore forgiveness as a transformative journey, looking into its psychological and emotional effects on individuals and its profound impact on mental health, physical health, and social dynamics.

In this part of the book, I will discuss practical strategies for cultivating forgiveness and its potential to promote personal growth, reconciliation within ourselves, and a more compassionate society, which is much needed today.

Below, I would like to quote five simple reasons why it is essential to let go.

- *The past is in the past; we cannot change what is done. As quoted before,* ***we need to stop hoping for a better past. Dr Fred Luskin***

- *When you let go, you create space for something new: this one is one of the most powerful as it shows us what the future could look like.*

- *Your past does not define you. We are ever-evolving beings, so our future is not limited by what we have done or have gone through in our past.*

- *Our Self-limiting beliefs are what hold us back from letting go and growing.*

- *Letting go is the foundation of change, an inevitable part of life.*

The process of forgiving, not forgetting.

Forgiveness can be directed inwardly as a means of self-healing and outwardly as a means of reconciling with others. In this chapter, I would like to explore forgiveness as a form of healing, emphasising its capacity to transform lives and promote holistic well-being.

Forgiving and forgetting are two distinct concepts, and understanding the difference between them is crucial when recovering from abuse.

Forgiving involves a deliberate and conscious decision to let go of anger, resentment, and the desire for revenge toward the person who harmed you. It is a process of releasing negative emotions and granting pardon or absolution to the perpetrator. Forgiveness can be a deeply personal and therapeutic act. Still, it does not necessarily require or imply forgetting the past or condoning abusive behaviour.

On the other hand, forgetting involves erasing or suppressing memories of a traumatic event. It means intentionally putting the memory out of one's mind or experiencing memory loss related to the traumatic experience. Forgetting is not always a conscious choice, and it can occur as a defence mechanism to protect oneself from the pain of the trauma.

The Importance of Understanding these concepts in recovery from abuse:

Empowerment: Understanding the difference between forgiving and forgetting can empower abuse survivors. They may feel pressured to forgive their abusers as a way of moving forward. Still, it's essential to recognise that forgiveness is personal and should not be rushed or forced.

Acknowledging the Pain: Forgiveness does not require survivors to deny or suppress their pain. It's possible to forgive while recognising the harm and suffering experienced; this can be a healthy way to process the trauma. Recognising that forgiveness and forgetting are separate allows survivors to set boundaries. They can choose to forgive without allowing the abusive person back into their life or without excusing the behaviour.

Personal Healing: Forgiveness can be a part of the healing process, but it's not the same as healing. Survivors can work on healing and personal growth while deciding whether to forgive.

Emotional Safety: Forgetting can be a defence mechanism, but it may not be healthy or sustainable. Suppressing memories can lead to unresolved trauma and emotional distress. Understanding the difference between forgiving and forgetting can help survivors seek more beneficial ways to cope and heal.

Survivors need to practice self-compassion and self-care throughout their recovery, acknowledging the trauma and their feelings without judgment and choosing what is best for their well-being.

In summary, forgiveness and forgetting are distinct processes, and survivors of abuse should understand that they have choices when it comes to dealing with their past. It's essential to prioritise healing, self-care, and self-compassion while making decisions about forgiveness, and survivors should never feel pressured to forget or forgive as a means of coping with their trauma. Recovery is a deeply personal journey, and each survivor's path is unique.

Letting go of anger and resentment.

Letting go of anger and resentment as a survivor of abuse can be an essential aspect of the healing process, and here is why it's important:

Emotional Well-being: Holding onto anger and resentment can significantly affect your emotional well-being. These emotions can lead to persistent stress, anxiety, and even depression. Letting go allows you to experience greater emotional peace and freedom.

Physical Health: Chronic anger and resentment can adversely affect your physical health, including high blood pressure, heart problems, and compromised immune function, making you vulnerable to chronic autoimmune diseases. Releasing these emotions can contribute to better physical health.

Personal Growth: Releasing anger and resentment can create space for personal growth and self-improvement. It allows you to focus on healing, self-compassion, and building a positive future rather than being consumed by negative emotions.

Reduced Stress: Anger and resentment often lead to heightened stress levels. By letting go of these emotions, you can reduce stress and its associated adverse effects on your mind and body.

Improved Relationships: Carrying anger and resentment can affect your relationships with others. These emotions can make trusting, connecting, and forming healthy bonds with people challenging. Letting go of these feelings can lead to more positive and fulfilling relationships.

Empowerment: Letting go of anger and resentment can be an empowering choice. It shifts the focus from the abuser to your healing and well-being, allowing you to reclaim your power.

Emotional Freedom: Releasing anger and resentment frees you from the emotional burden of the past. It allows you to move forward without being weighed down by negative emotions from the abuse.

Self-Compassion: Releasing anger and resentment is an act of self-compassion. It involves treating yourself with kindness and understanding, acknowledging that you deserve to live a life free from the emotional shackles of the past.

Healing Trauma: Letting go of anger and resentment is an integral part of healing from the trauma of abuse. It allows you to process your feelings healthily and work through the emotional wounds left by the abuse.

Enhanced Resilience: You become more resilient as you let go of anger and resentment. You develop the capacity to cope with future challenges and stressors more healthily and adaptively.

It's important to note that letting go of anger and resentment does not mean forgetting or condoning the abuse. It is a process that can take time and often involves seeking support from therapists, counsellors, or support groups. Healing from abuse is a journey, and the path to letting go of these negative emotions may vary from person to person. Ultimately, it is a step toward reclaiming your life and moving forward in a healthier and more positive direction.

The Psychological Journey of Forgiveness

The acknowledgment and acceptance of the hurt and the pain caused by the relationship we have with these toxic people is the beginning of the psychological journey of forgiveness. We must allow ourselves to be vulnerable to recognise the emotional pain and suffering caused by a transgression. Acknowledging this pain is a crucial first step toward healing, as it allows us to confront our emotions and start letting go.

For a person who has been a victim of abuse, I know this could be a difficult step, as there is concern that by doing this, they could allow the perpetrators to repeat their actions, but this is not the case. Allowing ourselves to become vulnerable may make us feel uncomfortable and exposed initially. Still, it is necessary to start the healing process. It is impossible to skip the step, as going through it is the quickest way to get to the end. At this point, it is crucial to understand that we need to do this within ourselves; it is for us to understand and acknowledge how we feel.

Empathy and Understanding: Forgiveness involves developing compassion and understanding toward the offender. This step is not about excusing or condoning the wrongdoing of the other person but about recognising the humanity of both the victim and the offender. It involves attempting to understand the perspective of the person who hurt you; this doesn't mean justifying or excusing their actions; instead, it's an effort to empathise with their circumstances, motivations, or the factors that might have contributed to their behaviour. This understanding can help you see the situation from a more well-rounded viewpoint.

Once you reach this point, it makes it easier to *Release the Desire for Revenge*. When you choose to forgive, you consciously relinquish the urge to seek retaliation or harm in return for the wrongdoing. Getting to this stage has been my gold as I now understand that this choice empowers me to break the cycle of negativity and retaliation. I have also realised that negativity is extremely energy-consuming, with no positive or helpful outcome.

The Emotional and Physiological Benefits of Forgiveness:

Emotional Healing and Inner Peace: Forgiveness is a step toward emotional healing. By choosing to forgive, you prioritise your emotional, psychological, and physical well-being over holding onto grudges. It doesn't mean you instantly feel better, but it starts the process of reducing emotional pain and cultivating inner peace. Studies have also proved that forgiveness is closely linked to reduced stress levels. When individuals hold onto grudges, they often experience chronic stress, which can lead to a range of physical and mental health issues. Forgiveness can help break this cycle.

Improved Mental Health: Forgiveness has a positive impact on mental health. Studies have shown that when individuals decide to forgive, they manifest lower levels of depression, anxiety, and anger, as well as establish better levels of emotional resilience and a greater sense of well-being.

Enhanced Physical Health: The health benefits of forgiveness extend to the body. Research suggests that forgiving individuals have lower blood pressure, reduced risk of heart disease, and a strengthened immune system. The mind-body connection plays a significant role in this phenomenon.

Forgiveness in Relationships Reconciliation: Although not for everyone, forgiveness can pave the way for reconciliation in damaged relationships. It fosters communication, understanding, and the possibility of rebuilding trust. It can also prevent resentment in ongoing relationships and the accumulation of resentment over time. It promotes healthier and more harmonious interactions.

Cultivating Compassion: Forgiving in relationships can also develop compassion, empathy, and a deeper understanding of one another; this can lead to more robust, more resilient bonds.

Practical Strategies for Cultivating Forgiveness

Self-Reflection: Start by reflecting on your feelings and emotions. Recognise the impact of holding onto grudges and the benefits of forgiveness for your well-being.

Empathy Development: Practice empathy by seeing the situation from the offender's perspective; this can help you better understand their motivations and actions.

Open and honest communication is essential. Express your feelings and thoughts and listen to the other person's perspective. However, remember that forgiveness does not necessarily mean reconciliation or maintaining a harmful relationship. It's important to set healthy boundaries when necessary.

In conclusion, forgiveness is a profound and transformative process that offers healing to those who embrace it. Its benefits extend to mental and physical health, as well as the dynamics of interpersonal relationships. As individuals, communities, and societies, we can harness forgiveness for healing, reconciliation, and a more compassionate world. By understanding the psychological journey of forgiveness and practising its principles, we can unlock its potential to heal wounds, mend relationships, and foster personal growth.

The decision to Forgive: Forgiveness is a conscious decision. It involves choosing to release negative emotions and resentment. This choice empowers individuals to take control of their emotional well-being.

Healing and Transformation: Individuals often experience emotional and personal transformation as forgiveness takes hold.

They may find relief from anger, anxiety, and depression. This process can increase self-esteem and a greater sense of inner peace.

Achieving Closure for Your Well-being

Achieving Closure can be an essential but complex concept when recovering from abuse. Its importance for an individual's well-being can vary depending on the person and the specific circumstances of the abuse. Here are some considerations:

Individual Variability: The need for Closure varies from person to person. Some individuals may find that achieving Closure is essential in their healing process. In contrast, others may not feel the same way. It's important to recognise and respect these individual differences.

What Closure Represents: Closure, in the context of abuse recovery, often represents a sense of resolution, understanding, or acceptance regarding the traumatic experience. It can involve acknowledging the impact of the abuse, coming to terms with it, and finding a way to move forward. Again, it is different for each individual.

Emotional Healing: Closure can contribute to emotional healing by providing a sense of finality or clarity about the past. It may help individuals process their feelings and release lingering emotional pain.

Empowerment: Achieving Closure can be an empowering experience. It may involve taking control of one's narrative, setting boundaries, or making choices that prioritise personal well-being and healing.

Preventing Rumination: In some cases, the absence of Closure can lead to rumination, where individuals repeatedly think about and obsess over abusive experiences. Closure can help interrupt this cycle and reduce the emotional distress associated with intrusive thoughts.

Moving Forward: Closure can signify the readiness to move forward in life, to focus on personal growth, and to engage in new relationships and experiences without being unduly burdened by the past.

Forgiveness and Letting Go: For some survivors, achieving closure may involve forgiving the abuser or finding a way to let go of resentment. Forgiveness can be a powerful act of self-compassion and healing, but it's unnecessary for everyone's recovery.

It's essential to emphasise that Closure is a highly individualised and personal process. Not all survivors of abuse will feel the need or readiness for Closure, and that's perfectly valid. Some survivors may find Closure through therapy, support groups, self-reflection, or even by finding ways to advocate for others who have experienced similar trauma.

Moreover, Closure may not always result in complete resolution or neatly tied-up loose ends. Trauma recovery can be complex, and it often involves ongoing self-care, self-compassion, and support from mental health professionals or support networks.

Ultimately, the most crucial aspect of recovery from abuse is prioritising one's own well-being, safety, and healing journey, whether or not it involves achieving Closure in the traditional sense.

Dear Reader,

Thank you for choosing "Healing the Past", a book designed to help you understand and overcome the effects of emotionally immature, toxic, and abusive experiences.

Your feedback matters to me, as I aim to extend this message to many other people who could benefit from it! I invite you to share your thoughts and insights on "Healing the Past" by leaving a review so I can make this happen. Your review will help others and guide my efforts to support more individuals on their healing journey.

Get that 'feel good' feeling of helping other people for real, simply scan the QR code below to leave your review:

I'm so excited to share with you all the strategies and techniques that help me to overcome these experiences in the coming chapters.

Thank you for joining me on this transformative path towards healing.

Yours sincerely, Norma

CHAPTER 6 STEP 6

The Healing Journey

Self Forgiveness

The journey to self-forgiveness for a survivor of abuse can be an incredibly complex and challenging path. It involves acknowledging and processing a range of emotions, including guilt, shame, anger, and often deep-seated feelings of unworthiness that the abuser may have instilled.

Some aspects of what this journey might entail are:

Acknowledgment and Acceptance: It starts with recognising that you were a victim of abuse and understanding that it was not your fault. Accepting this reality is a crucial step towards self-forgiveness.

Processing Emotions: Allowing yourself to feel and express emotions associated with the abuse—anger, grief, sadness, and more—is essential for healing. Suppressing these emotions can hinder progress toward self-forgiveness.

Shifting Blame: Often, survivors may blame themselves for the abuse or feel responsible in some way. Learning to shift the blame away from oneself and towards the abuser is essential and liberating in the journey towards self-forgiveness.

Self-Compassion: Developing self-compassion involves treating oneself with kindness, understanding, and patience, similar to supporting a friend through a difficult time.

Seeking Support: Engaging with a therapist, counsellor, support group, or trusted individuals who can provide guidance, validation, and support throughout this journey is incredibly helpful. They can offer perspectives that aid in reframing thoughts and emotions.

Reframing Beliefs: Often, survivors hold beliefs about themselves that were imposed by the abuser, such as being unworthy or deserving of mistreatment. Replacing these beliefs with positive, affirming thoughts is crucial

Letting Go of Perfection: Self-forgiveness involves understanding that it's okay to make mistakes, to have vulnerabilities, and to be imperfect. Embracing imperfection is part of self-acceptance, and establishing healthy boundaries in relationships, including the relationship with oneself, is essential for self-protection and self-respect.

Patience and Time: Self-forgiveness is a process that takes time and patience. It's not a linear journey, and setbacks may occur. Being patient with oneself through the ups and downs is crucial.

Reclaiming Personal Power: Rediscovering one's strength, Resilience, and personal power is a significant part of the journey. It involves regaining a sense of control over one's life and choices.

It's important to note again that self-forgiveness doesn't mean forgetting or excusing what happened. It's about releasing the burden of self-blame and allowing oneself to heal and move forward despite the past. The journey is unique to each survivor, and it's essential to approach it at one's own pace, with self-care and compassion.

The key to healthy relationships

A combination of self-healing and consciously cultivating healthy relationship dynamics are some of the essential principles and strategies for building and keeping healthy relationships after abuse.

Self-Healing and Self-Understanding: it is vital to take the responsibility to embark on a journey of self-healing and self-discovery. Understanding one's wounds, triggers, and emotional responses is crucial for building healthier relationships and exploring our past experiences and the impact of abuse on our self-esteem, self-worth, and attachment style. This self-awareness is the foundation for personal growth.

Establishing Boundaries: As we stated before learning the importance of setting and maintaining boundaries in relationships is vital. We need to learn to see boundaries as a sign of self-respect and self-care, identifying our boundaries and communicating them assertively to the people around us, as well as respecting the boundaries of others is essential.

Effective Communication: the significance of open, honest, and respectful communication in healthy relationships is vital. Help develop communication skills that promote understanding and empathy. Address any communication patterns created as a result of abuse, such as avoidance or aggressive behaviour, and work on healthier alternatives.

Building Trust Gradually: Understanding that trust may have been lost by past abuse and rebuilding it gradually, both in ourselves and in the people around us, is the only way to regain this. Remembering the importance of consistency, reliability, and transparency in fostering trust in relationships is also vital.

Healthy Conflict Resolution: We must educate ourselves about healthy conflict resolution strategies. Disagreements are standard but can be resolved constructively without resorting to abusive behaviours. Learning to manage our emotions during conflicts and to seek compromise and solutions that benefit both parties is vital.

Recognising Red Flags: Recognising red flags of potentially abusive relationship behaviour is an essential skill to develop. It is vital to trust our instincts and seek help or distance ourselves from unhealthy situations that arise. Early intervention and boundary-setting when encountering problematic behaviours in new relationships are crucial.

Self-Care and Self-Compassion: Emphasise the importance of self-care and self-compassion is fundamental. Prioritising our well-being, physical and emotional health, and self-esteem will help us to develop self-compassion as a countermeasure to any lingering shame or self-blame resulting from past abuse.

Seeking support through therapy, support groups, or trusted friends and family members would be very beneficial. A supportive network can provide validation and guidance. Highlight that seeking professional help is a sign of strength, not weakness, and can significantly aid healing and growth.

Take time for Self-Reflection: Engaging periodically in self-reflection to assess the health of our relationships and personal development would be very helpful. Self-reflection can help understand and identify areas for improvement and celebrate successes.

Embracing Growth and Transformation: It is important to remember that healing from past abuse is an ongoing process, so to embrace growth and transformation and see ourselves as survivors who can build healthier, more fulfilling relationships is fundamental.

In conclusion, the key to healthy relationships after abuse involves a combination of self-healing, self-awareness, and the cultivation of healthy relationship skills. Embarking on this journey to empower ourselves to build and sustain relationships founded on respect, trust, and mutual well-being should be our primary goal.

Healthy relationships are attainable for survivors of abuse. With the proper guidance and commitment to personal growth, we can create fulfilling and nurturing connections with others.

Self-compassion: The cornerstone of healing

As previously discussed, Self-compassion is treating oneself with the same kindness, understanding, and care that one would offer a close friend or loved one in times of suffering or difficulty. It involves acknowledging one's pain, flaws, and imperfections without judgment and responding with gentleness and empathy.

There are three critical components to Self-compassion.

Self-Kindness: This involves being understanding and gentle with oneself rather than critical and judgmental. Instead of harsh self-criticism, self-kindness encourages self-soothing and self-nurturing.

Common Humanity: Recognising that suffering, imperfection, and difficulties are part of the human experience. Instead of feeling isolated in one's struggles, self-compassion reminds us that we are not alone in facing challenges; others are going through similar challenges.

Mindfulness: Practicing mindfulness involves being aware of one's thoughts and feelings without over-identifying with them. It's about maintaining a balanced perspective on oneself and one's experiences, being present and fully engaged in the current moment, and acknowledging thoughts, feelings, and the surrounding environment without judgment.

The reason why Self-compassion is considered the cornerstone of healing is that it reduces Self-Criticism. Many individuals who have experienced trauma, abuse, or complex life events tend to be very self-critical. Self-compassion counters this harsh self-judgment by encouraging a more forgiving and understanding attitude toward oneself; this can help break the cycle of shame and self-blame.

Self-compassion also promotes Emotional Healing, allowing individuals to process and heal emotional wounds. By acknowledging and validating their pain, survivors of trauma can work through their feelings more healthily. It enhances Resilience by providing a solid foundation of self-support. When facing challenging situations, individuals with self-compassion are more likely to respond with self-care and self-kindness, which helps them cope better with adversity.

Improves Self-Esteem: Self-compassion is associated with higher self-esteem. It helps individuals recognise their worthiness and value as human beings, irrespective of their past experiences or perceived flaws.

It encourages seeking help; people with self-compassion are more likely to seek professional help and support when needed. They understand the importance of self-care and recognise that reaching out for assistance is a compassionate act toward themselves.

Reduces Perfectionism, many survivors of trauma or abuse may struggle with perfectionism, trying to control everything to avoid further harm. Self-compassion helps individuals accept their imperfections and understand they need not be perfect to deserve care and love.

Fosters a Sense of Safety: Self-compassion creates a sense of emotional safety. Survivors of trauma often have difficulty feeling safe in the world or their bodies. Self-compassion can help individuals feel safer and more secure within themselves.

In essence, self-compassion is a vital psychological resource that can help individuals navigate the challenging journey of healing from trauma, abuse, or other difficult life experiences. It provides the foundation for self-support, self-care, and self-acceptance, allowing survivors to achieve greater well-being and resilience.

Building Resilience and inner strength

As we now know recovering from a relationship with emotionally immature and abusive parents can be a challenging and emotionally taxing journey. However, building resilience and inner strength is possible with time, effort, and support.

Steps to help you in this process are:

Educate Yourself: Understanding the dynamics of emotionally immature and abusive relationships can be empowering. Books, articles, and resources on the subject can help you make sense of your experiences and realise that you are not alone.

Establish Boundaries: Learning to set and stay firm when setting healthy boundaries is crucial. This includes boundaries with your parents and other people in your life; they will protect your emotional well-being and help you maintain a sense of control in your day-to-day.

Prioritise self-care practices that promote physical and emotional well-being, including exercise, meditation, journaling, hobbies, and spending time with supportive friends and loved ones.

Build a Support Network, surrounding yourself with people who understand and support you; this includes friends, family members, support groups, or online communities. Sharing your experiences and feelings with supportive individuals can be incredibly validating and healing.

Process Your Emotions Freely, give yourself permission to feel and express your emotions; this may involve journaling, art, or talking with a friend you trust. Feelings suppressed or denied need to be acknowledged and processed for healing.

Practice Self-Compassion: recognising that healing from an abusive relationship takes time is essential, and setbacks are normal. Always treat yourself with the same understanding you would offer a friend in a similar situation.

Challenge Negative Beliefs: emotional abuse often leaves survivors with negative beliefs about themselves. Work on challenging and reframing these beliefs with the help of a therapist or through self-reflection.

Set Goals: Define your personal goals and aspirations. Focus on what you want to achieve and work towards those goals. Building a future that aligns with your values and desires can motivate and empower you. Practising Mindfulness techniques will help you stay in the present moment and reduce anxiety or rumination about the past. Deep breathing exercises and mindful meditation can also be beneficial.

Create a Safe Space: establishing a safe and supportive physical and emotional environment for yourself is vital; this may involve distancing yourself from toxic relationships or creating a calming and nurturing space at home.

Seek Professional Help: Working with a professional therapist or counsellor specialising in trauma, abuse, and family issues could be significant, as a professional can provide support, guidance, and coping strategies tailored to your situation.

Consider No Contact: this is a tough decision to take, but in some cases, maintaining no contact with emotionally abusive parents may be necessary or the only option for our well-being. I know this may sound selfish to some people as we are talking about our parents, but sometimes there is no other way.

In my case, I have learned that having a relationship with my parents would have cost me my marriage and my family and would have put me in financial ruin; and this is because, in my mother's world, I do not exist as an individual; in her world, I am an extension of her as a person, like a puppet, and not complying with this would have been incomprehensible to my mother. Unfortunately, my father followed along with anything my mother's wanted or said. However, this is a critical decision and must not be made lightly; the guidance of a therapist or counsellor would be of great help at this point, but ultimately, the decision would be yours.

Remember, healing from an emotionally abusive relationship with your parents is a unique and personal journey. It may involve ups and downs, but you can build Resilience and Inner Strength with time and effort. Seek professional help when needed, rely on your support network, and prioritise self-care and self-compassion throughout your recovery process would be vital.

Therapeutic techniques for processing trauma.

Here are ten therapeutic techniques that can be effective for processing trauma. These techniques are often used by mental health professionals, including therapists, counsellors, and psychologists, in their work with individuals who have experienced trauma:

Cognitive-Behavioural Therapy (CBT):

CBT helps individuals identify and question negative beliefs and unhealthy patterns of trauma. It assists in reframing these thoughts and developing healthier coping strategies. Cognitive-behavioural Therapy (CBT) is an evidence-based psychotherapeutic approach that focuses on helping individuals identify and change unhelpful thought patterns and behaviours. It is often employed to address various mental health issues, including depression, phobias, anxiety disorders, post-traumatic stress disorder, and many other conditions.

CBT is based on the principle that our feelings, thoughts, and behaviours are interconnected and that by modifying negative thought patterns and maladaptive behaviours, the person can improve their emotional well-being and overall mental health.

The fundamental principles of CBT include:

Cognitive Restructuring: CBT helps individuals identify and challenge irrational or negative thought patterns (cognitive distortions) contributing to emotional distress. Individuals can change their emotional responses by replacing these with more balanced and realistic thoughts.

Behavioural Techniques: CBT employs various strategies to help individuals change their behaviour and develop healthier coping skills; this might involve *Exposure Therapy*, where individuals gradually face their fears, or behaviour modification techniques that encourage positive behaviours and discourage negative ones.

Collaboration: The therapist and the individual work together collaboratively to set goals, develop strategies, and monitor progress. This partnership is essential to the success of CBT.

Problem-Solving: CBT teaches individuals problem-solving skills, helping them deal with challenges and conflicts more effectively; this includes homework assignments, which encourage individuals to practice the skills they've learned in Therapy in real-life situations.

CBT is typically a short-term, goal-oriented therapy with a specific focus on addressing the immediate issues that the individual is facing. It is highly structured, and sessions are usually conducted regularly. CBT is effective in treating many psychological disorders and is often used either alone or in combination with other therapeutic approaches or medications.

It's important to note that in CBT the specific techniques and strategies used can be tailored to an individual's unique needs and circumstances. Additionally, CBT is typically administered by trained mental health professionals, such as licensed therapists, psychiatrists, or psychologists.

Eye Movement Desensitization and Reprocessing (EMDR):

EMDR is a specialised therapy that uses bilateral stimulation to process traumatic memories. It is a psychotherapeutic approach and therapeutic technique designed to help individuals process and resolve distressing or traumatic memories, reducing the emotional and psychological impact of these experiences. Francine Shapiro developed EMDR in the late 1980s and has since gained popularity and respect as an effective way of treatment for conditions such as post-traumatic stress disorder (PTSD), as well as other psychological and emotional difficulties.

The critical components of EMDR include:

Bilateral Stimulation: EMDR involves a structured approach in which the therapist guides the individual through a series of bilateral stimulation, which can be in the form of side-to-side eye movements, auditory tones, or tactile sensations (e.g., tapping or hand gestures). This bilateral stimulation mimics the rapid eye movement (REM) phase of sleep, during this time the brain processes and reorganises information.

Targeting Disturbing Memories: In EMDR therapy, the individual identifies specific traumatic or distressing memories that are causing emotional distress or dysfunction. These memories are then targeted for desensitisation and reprocessing: While revisiting the uncomfortable memory, the individual follows the therapist's guidance in focusing on the memory and its associated thoughts, emotions, and physical sensations. The bilateral stimulation facilitates processing these elements, aiming to reduce the distress and emotional charge associated with the memory.

Adaptive Resolution: The goal of EMDR is to help the individual reach an adaptive resolution of the traumatic memory, where the memory remains a part of their past but no longer triggers intense emotional distress or disruptive symptoms. This process results in a more balanced and less distressing perspective on the memory.

EMDR is typically administered by trained therapists who follow a standardised protocol. The number of sessions required can vary depending on the individual and the nature of the trauma or distressing memory being addressed.

While EMDR has gained recognition as an effective treatment for trauma-related conditions, it is essential to note that its mechanisms are still a subject of ongoing research and debate. Patients who have undergone this treatment have reported positive outcomes and symptom relief with EMDR therapy. It is important to seek a qualified and licensed therapist if you are interested in EMDR, as the technique requires specialised training and expertise.

Narrative Therapy:

This Therapy encourages individuals to tell their trauma stories in a safe and structured environment. It helps individuals make sense of their experiences and view themselves as survivors rather than victims. Narrative Therapy is a form of psychotherapy that explores and reshapes individuals' stories about their lives. It was developed by Michael White and David Epston in the 1980s and is rooted in the belief that our identities and experiences are shaped by the narratives or stories we construct about ourselves, our relationships, and the world around us.

Fundamental principles and components of Narrative Therapy include:

Externalisation: Narrative therapy helps individuals externalise their problems, separating the issue or challenge from their sense of self. By doing so, individuals can view the issue as an external force rather than an inherent aspect of their identity.

Reauthoring Stories: In this therapeutic approach, individuals are encouraged to "reauthor" their life narratives by challenging and re-evaluating the dominant stories that may be causing distress or dysfunction. It empowers them to construct alternative, more positive narratives that align with their values and preferred identities.

Deconstruction of Dominant Narratives: Narrative therapists work with clients to deconstruct the dominant or problematic stories they have constructed, which often involve negative self-perceptions, self-blame, or feelings of powerlessness. By critically examining these narratives, individuals can gain new perspectives and insights.

Collaborative Approach: Narrative therapy is a collaborative and client-centred approach. Therapists work with individuals to help them explore their experiences and identify the preferred stories they want to embrace.

Cultural and Contextual Considerations: Narrative therapy recognises the influence of cultural and social contexts on forming individual narratives and identities. It encourages individuals to consider how societal norms and cultural factors may impact their stories. Narrative Therapy may involve external witnesses, such as family members or friends, who can help validate and support the new narratives and perspectives being developed in treatment.

Narrative Therapy is commonly used to address issues like anxiety, depression, trauma, family conflicts, and relationship problems but is not limited to these. It is precious in empowering individuals to reframe their experiences and regain a sense of agency in their lives. Therapists who practice Narrative Therapy typically engage in conversations with their clients, asking open-ended questions and actively listening to help individuals explore their stories, discover alternative interpretations, and work toward a more constructive and empowering self-narrative.

Mindfulness-Based Stress Reduction (MBSR):

MBSR combines mindfulness meditation and body awareness techniques to help individuals stay present in the moment, reducing the emotional charge of traumatic memories. It is a structured and evidence-based program that combines mindfulness meditation and awareness techniques with elements of Cognitive Therapy. It is designed to improve the overall well-being of individuals by reducing anxiety, managing stress, and cultivating mindfulness, which involves non-judgmental awareness of the present moment.

Key features of MBSR include:

Mindfulness Meditation: MBSR incorporates mindfulness meditation practices, such as body scanning, breath awareness, and mindfulness of thoughts and emotions. These techniques motivate individuals to become more attuned to their physical sensations, ideas, and feelings as they arise in the present moment.

Stress Reduction: MBSR aims to teach participants how to respond to stress more adaptively and less reactively. By developing mindfulness skills, individuals can better manage the physical and emotional effects of stress.

Cognitive and Behavioural Approaches: While rooted in mindfulness, MBSR also includes elements of Cognitive Therapy, which help individuals recognise and challenge unhelpful thought patterns that contribute to stress and anxiety. Combining mindfulness and cognitive techniques empowers individuals to change their responses to stressors.

Group Format: MBSR programs are often conducted in a group setting, led by a trained MBSR instructor. Group sessions typically span several weeks, during which participants practice mindfulness exercises and discuss their experiences with fellow group members. Individuals are encouraged to engage in daily mindfulness outside group sessions to reinforce their skills and incorporate mindfulness into their daily lives.

Dr. Jon Kabat-Zinn developed MBSR in the late 1970s, and it has since gained recognition for its effectiveness in reducing stress, improving emotional well-being, and enhancing overall quality of life. While it was initially developed to address stress, MBSR has been adapted and applied to conditions including anxiety, depression, chronic pain, and various medical and psychological issues. The practice of MBSR can be a valuable tool for individuals seeking to enhance their self-awareness, develop better coping strategies for stress, and lead a more balanced and mindful life. Trained MBSR instructors typically teach it, and it is accessible to people from various backgrounds and age groups.

Dialectical Behaviour Therapy (DBT):

DBT combines elements of cognitive-behavioural Therapy with mindfulness techniques. It assists individuals in regulating their emotions, improving interpersonal skills, and managing distress. DBT is a specialised cognitive-behavioural treatment Dr. Marsha Linehan developed in the late 20th century. DBT is designed to help individuals who experience intense emotional and behavioural challenges, particularly those with borderline personality disorder (BPD). However, it has also proven effective for a range of other mental health conditions.

Key components of DBT include:

Dialectical Approach: The term "dialectical" in DBT refers to the balance between two seemingly opposing principles: acceptance and change. DBT teaches individuals to accept themselves and their current situation while also working to change problematic behaviours and emotional responses. It emphasises the synthesis of these two concepts to promote personal growth.

Mindfulness: DBT strongly emphasises mindfulness practices, which involve being fully present and aware of the moment without judgment. Mindfulness skills help individuals observe and regulate their emotions and reactions more effectively.

Emotion Regulation: DBT provides strategies and techniques to help individuals identify, understand, and manage their intense and potentially destructive emotions. These skills empower individuals to regulate emotional responses and make healthier choices.

Interpersonal Effectiveness: DBT helps individuals improve their interpersonal and Communication skills. It focuses on building and maintaining healthy relationships, setting boundaries, and resolving conflicts.

Distress Tolerance: DBT teaches individuals how to cope with distressing situations and crises without resorting to self-destructive or impulsive behaviours; this includes learning to tolerate discomfort and pain when necessary.

Individual and Group Therapy: DBT is typically delivered through group skills training and individual therapy sessions. The group component provides a supportive environment for individuals to learn and practice DBT skills.

DBT is often used for individuals who struggle with emotional dysregulation, self-harm, suicidal thoughts, impulsive behaviour, and difficulties in relationships. It is a comprehensive and structured approach to Therapy, and therapists who practice DBT undergo specialised training to provide this treatment. While initially developed for borderline personality disorder, DBT has been adapted and proven effective for other conditions, such as eating disorders, movement disorders, and substance use disorders. It has become one of the leading approaches in the field of psychotherapy for individuals with complex emotional and behavioural challenges.

Art Therapy:

Art therapy allows individuals to express and process their trauma through various artistic mediums, such as drawing, painting, or sculpture; this can be particularly helpful for those who struggle to verbalise their experiences. Art therapy is a therapeutic approach that utilises the process of making art to help survivors express their thoughts, emotions, and experiences through their creative Expression. It involves the use of various art materials, such as paints, clay, and drawing tools, to facilitate self-exploration and personal growth under the guidance of a trained art therapist.

Key features of art therapy include:

Creative Expression: Art therapy encourages individuals to use artistic materials and techniques to convey their inner feelings and thoughts in a non-verbal and symbolic way; this allows for expressing complex emotions that may be challenging to articulate verbally.

Self-Exploration: Through creating art, individuals can gain insights into their inner world, develop self-awareness, and gain a deeper understanding of their concerns, conflicts, and personal narratives.

Therapeutic Relationship: Art therapy is often conducted in a therapeutic setting with a qualified art therapist who guides and supports individuals as they create art and explore the meaning behind their creations. The therapeutic relationship is a crucial part of the process.

Integration of Mind and Body: Creating art engages the mind and the body, providing a holistic approach to self-expression and healing. It can be especially favourable for individuals who find traditional talk therapy more challenging.

Symbolism and Metaphor: Artistic images and symbols can serve as metaphors for inner experiences and can be used to explore unconscious or deep-seated emotions and issues.

Art therapy is used to address a wide variety of emotional and psychological challenges, including but not limited to anxiety, depression, trauma, stress, and relationship issues. Art therapy can be adapted to each individual's unique needs and abilities, making it a versatile and inclusive form of treatment. It can be an extraordinary tool for healing, self-expression, personal growth, and healing, and it complements traditional talk therapy approaches by offering alternative ways to access and process emotions and experiences.

Somatic Experiencing (SE):

SE focuses on the body's physical sensations and reactions to trauma. It helps individuals release stored tension and trauma-related physical symptoms through gentle movement and awareness exercises. It is designed to address and heal the physical and psychological effects of trauma, stress, and overwhelming life experiences. Developed by Dr. Peter A. Levine, SE is based on the understanding that trauma can become trapped in the body and that the body's natural healing capacities can be harnessed to release and resolve these traumatic imprints.

Key elements of Somatic Experiencing include:

Body Awareness: Somatic Experiencing places a strong emphasis on body awareness, helping individuals become more attuned to the physical sensations, responses, and tension held in the body as a result of trauma or stress.

Resourcing and Titration: Titration is a gradual and careful approach to exploring and processing difficult or traumatic experiences and sensations to prevent overwhelming. In SE, clients learn to identify and engage with their internal and external resources, which can provide safety and support during the therapeutic process.

Pendulation: SE recognises the importance of the body's natural rhythm and ability to move between states of tension and relaxation. Pendulation therapy guides individuals to notice this pendulation, facilitating the release of stored trauma energy.

Completing the Survival Response: SE focuses on helping individuals achieve instinctual survival responses that were interrupted during a traumatic event; this allows the body to discharge the stored energy associated with the uncompleted response.

Mind-Body Connection: The approach acknowledges the interconnectedness of the mind and body and emphasises the importance of addressing both in the healing process.

Somatic Experiencing is commonly used to address the effects of acute and chronic trauma, including post-traumatic stress disorder (PTSD), and it is also applied to other conditions involving stress and anxiety. It is typically administered by certified SE practitioners with specialised training in this approach. Somatic Experiencing promotes healing, Resilience, and well-being by helping individuals release trauma's physical and emotional residues and restore a sense of safety, balance, and vitality. It offers a non-intrusive and client-centred approach to trauma therapy, focusing on the individual's unique experience and needs.

Group Therapy:

Group Therapy is a form of psychotherapy in which a small group of individuals with similar concerns or issues come together, guided by a trained therapist, to share experiences, provide support, and work collaboratively to address emotional and psychological challenges. It offers a supportive and interactive environment for participants to gain insight, receive feedback, and develop coping skills within a group setting. Group therapy provides a supportive and validating environment where individuals can share their experiences, learn from others, and create a sense of belonging. Group members often offer valuable insights and empathy.

Trauma-Informed Yoga:

TIY is a specialised approach to yoga practice that recognises and addresses the physical, emotional, and psychological effects of trauma. It is guided by the principles of safety, choice, and empowerment, with a strong emphasis on creating a supportive and non-triggering environment for individuals who have experienced trauma. Trauma-informed yoga instructors are trained to offer modifications and adaptations to traditional yoga poses and practices, prioritising the well-being and comfort of participants. This approach aims to help individuals with trauma histories develop greater self-awareness, Resilience, and a sense of control over their bodies and emotions through the practice of yoga. It combines yoga postures, breathing exercises, and mindfulness to help individuals reconnect with their bodies in a safe and non-threatening way. It can aid in restoring a sense of bodily safety and control.

Key components of Trauma-Informed Yoga include:

Safety: Ensuring physical and emotional safety is paramount. The yoga instructor creates a safe space where participants can practice without fear of judgment, re-traumatisation, or emotional distress; this includes establishing clear boundaries, confidentiality, and a non-coercive atmosphere.

Choice and Empowerment: Participants are encouraged to make choices that feel right for them throughout the practice. They can decide whether to perform specific poses, modify, or rest when needed; this empowers individuals to take control over their own experiences.

Mindful Awareness: Trauma-Informed Yoga places a strong emphasis on mindfulness, encouraging participants to stay present in the moment, connect with their bodies, and observe their thoughts and sensations without judgment. Mindfulness practices help individuals develop self-awareness and self-regulation skills.

Gentle and Non-Triggering Approach: The yoga instructor offers gentle, non-triggering cues and language, avoiding forceful or aggressive adjustments. The emphasis is on compassion and self-compassion.

Modifications and Adaptations: Trauma-informed yoga instructors are trained to offer various pose modifications and adaptations to accommodate individual needs and comfort levels; this may include props, variations, and alternative poses to make the practice accessible to all.

Grounding Techniques: Incorporating grounding techniques and exercises can help participants reconnect with their bodies and create a sense of stability and safety. These techniques may include deep breathing, body scanning, and gentle movements.

Supportive Community: Group dynamics in Trauma-Informed Yoga can foster a sense of connection and community among participants, which can be healing for individuals who may have experienced isolation or disconnection due to trauma.

Understanding Trauma: Trauma-Informed Yoga instructors are trained to have a basic understanding of trauma and its effects, including how it can manifest physically and emotionally. This knowledge helps them respond empathetically and appropriately to participants' needs.

Trauma-informed yoga is not a one-size-fits-all approach, and instructors adapt their teaching to accommodate participants' unique needs and experiences. This approach is often used in a variety of settings, including mental health clinics, addiction recovery programs, and community organisations, to help individuals build Resilience, self-regulation, and a positive relationship with their bodies and emotions.

It's important to note that the choice of therapeutic technique should be based on an individual's specific needs and preferences. Trauma therapy is highly individualised, and what works best for one person may not be as effective for another. Additionally, these techniques are often combined, and therapists may tailor their approach to meet each patient's needs.

Journaling and self-reflection exercises

Journaling and self-reflection exercises can be incredibly effective and valuable components of the recovery process for survivors of abuse, and some of the reasons why are:

Emotional Expression: Journaling provides a safe and private space for survivors to express their emotions. It allows them to put their thoughts and feelings into words, which can be a cathartic and validating experience.

Self-Exploration: Through journaling and self-reflection, survivors can explore their inner thoughts, beliefs, and reactions and gain a deeper understanding of themselves and their responses to past trauma.

Processing Trauma: Writing about traumatic experiences can assist survivors in processing and making sense of what happened. It can help them untangle complex emotions and find a narrative that makes sense to them.

Tracking Progress: Journaling allows survivors to track their progress over time. They can look back on their entries and see how they've grown and changed as they recover.

Setting Goals: Journaling can be a tool for developing and tracking personal goals. Survivors can document their healing journey, set achievable milestones, and celebrate their successes.

Identifying Triggers: Self-reflection helps survivors identify triggers or situations that may bring up difficult emotions or memories. This awareness is crucial for developing coping strategies and avoiding re-traumatisation.

Promoting Self-Compassion: Journaling can allow survivors to practice self-compassion and self-care. It will enable them to be gentle with themselves and acknowledge their progress and efforts.

Communication with Therapists: Journal entries can be valuable tools for therapists or counsellors. Sharing journal entries can help therapists gain insight into a survivor's thoughts and feelings, enabling more targeted support.

Empowerment: Journaling and reflecting on one's experiences can be empowering. It allows survivors to reclaim their voices and narratives, moving from passive victims to active participants in their healing.

Stress Reduction: Writing about distressing experiences can be a way to reduce stress and anxiety. It can serve as a healthy outlet for emotions that might otherwise be overwhelming.

Validation: Self-reflection and journaling validate survivors' experiences. They send the message that what they went through matters, and their feelings are valid and deserving of attention.

Closure: For some survivors, journaling can be a step toward achieving closure; this has been the case for me. It helped me process and let go of painful memories and emotions associated with the abuse.

It's important to note that journaling and self-reflection should be done at a survivor's own pace and comfort level. There is no right or wrong way to journal, and individuals should feel free to write as much or as little as they want. Additionally, some survivors may benefit from professional guidance or Therapy alongside their journaling efforts to ensure they receive comprehensive support in their recovery journey.

Finding Meaning and Purpose

Reclaiming your identity and self-worth I'm not a therapist, but I can share some general strategies that help me and might help you on your journey to reclaiming your identity and self-worth after experiencing abuse from emotionally immature and toxic parents. It's important to note that healing from such experiences can be a long and challenging process, and seeking the advice of a mental health professional is highly recommended. That said, here are some steps you can consider:

Set Goals and Celebrate Achievements: Establish achievable short and long-term goals for your personal growth and healing. Celebrate your accomplishments, no matter how small they may seem.

Creative Expression: Explore creative outlets like art, writing, music, or any other form of self-expression. Creativity can be a powerful way to process emotions and regain a sense of self.

Positive Affirmations: Create a long list of positive affirmations that counteract the negative messages from your past. Repeat these affirmations daily to reinforce your self-worth.

Limit Contact or Establish No-Contact: Depending on your situation, you may need to limit or completely cut off contact with toxic family members for your well-being. This personal decision can be challenging but may be necessary for your healing.

Seek Legal Advice (if necessary): If the abuse involves legal issues such as financial manipulation or harassment, consult with an attorney to explore your options and protect your rights.

Join Support Groups: Consider joining support groups or online communities for abuse survivors. Sharing experiences with others who have had similar experiences can be empowering and validating.

Remember that healing from abuse is a gradual process, and it's okay to take your time. Seek professional guidance when needed, and prioritise your well-being above all else. Your identity and self-worth are worth reclaiming, and with time and effort, you can rebuild a healthier and happier life.

Pursuing personal passions and goals; Pursuing personal passions and goals is incredibly important for anyone. Still, it can be significant for survivors of abuse from emotionally immature and toxic parents. Here are some reasons why it's important:

Self-Empowerment: Pursuing your passions and goals can empower you and help you regain control over your life. It allows you to focus on what you want and what makes you happy rather than being defined by the past or the toxic dynamics you may have experienced.

Healing and Recovery: Engaging in activities that you are passionate about can be therapeutic. It can help you process your emotions, build self-esteem, and work through the trauma you may have experienced.

Identity Development: Your passions and goals are essential to who you are. They can help you develop and define your identity, separate from the negative influences of your parents; this can be crucial for building a healthier sense of self.

Distraction and Coping Mechanism: Pursuing your passions can be a healthy distraction from the negative thoughts and memories of your past experiences. It can also be a positive coping strategy for managing stress and anxiety.

Building a Supportive Network: Engaging in activities related to your passions and goals can help you connect with like-minded individuals with similar interests. Creating a supportive network of friends can be crucial for your emotional well-being.

Creating a Fulfilling Life: Pursuing personal passions and goals can lead to a more fulfilling and satisfying life. It allows you to set your path and prioritise your happiness rather than being controlled by past or toxic influences.

It's important to remember that healing from abuse is a complex and individual journey, and pursuing your passions and goals is just one part of that journey. Depending on the severity of the abuse and its impact on your life, you may also benefit from Therapy, support groups, and other resources to help you heal and move forward.

Additionally, be patient and compassionate with yourself as you work toward your goals. Recovery and personal growth take time, and it's okay to seek professional help if needed. Your happiness and well-being are worth the effort, and pursuing your passions can be a powerful tool in your healing process.

Turning adversity into strength

As a survivor, turning adversity into strength involves a multifaceted approach that addresses their emotional, psychological, and behavioural well-being.

Here are some critical pieces of advice and strategies to facilitate this process:

Acknowledge and Validate Emotions: acknowledge and validate your emotional responses to adversity. Allowing yourself to feel and express emotions such as sadness, anger, or fear is the first step in processing difficult experiences.

Develop Resilience: Build resilience by fostering adaptive coping mechanisms; this includes problem-solving skills, emotion regulation, and a growth mindset that views adversity as an opportunity for personal growth.

Reframe Negative Thoughts:

- Challenge and reframe negative or self-defeating thought patterns.

- Replace pessimistic thoughts with more positive and constructive ones.

- Remember to treat oneself with the same kindness and understanding that one would offer to a friend facing adversity.

Self-compassion can help you navigate challenges with more excellent self-care and self-acceptance. Remember to set achievable goals for yourself, even in adversity. Break down larger goals into smaller, manageable steps to maintain a sense of progress and accomplishment. Support from friends, family, or support groups will be essential. Connection with others can provide emotional validation, perspective, and a sense of belonging.

Narrative Therapy: Using narrative techniques can help you reframe your life stories. Focus on highlighting moments of Resilience, growth, and personal strength in your narrative. Learn from adversity, reflect on the lessons you've learned from challenging experiences, and how those lessons can contribute to personal growth.

Mindfulness and Self-Care: Introduce mindfulness practices and self-care routines to promote emotional regulation and reduce stress. A way to stay present and reduce rumination about past adversity is with mindfulness techniques.

Foster Meaning and Purpose: finding or creating meaning and purpose in your life, even in adversity; this can involve exploring values, passions, and goals that provide direction and fulfilment.

Positive Psychology Interventions: Implement positive psychology interventions, such as gratitude exercises or strengths-based approaches, to promote well-being and a positive outlook.

Patience and Self-Reflection: recognise that the process of turning adversity into strength is not linear. Self-reflection and ongoing growth are essential components of this journey.

Ultimately, turning adversity into power is highly individualised, and the strategies employed in the healing process will vary based on each person's unique experiences and needs.

CHAPTER 7

Parenting beyond the legacy

Breaking the cycle of emotional immaturity and abuse.

Parenting beyond the Legacy of Emotionally Immature and Abusive Parents: Parenting is a complex and multifaceted journey, influenced by many factors, including upbringing and family dynamics. When individuals have experienced emotionally immature or abusive parenting, breaking the cycle and nurturing healthy, loving relationships with their children can be challenging but not impossible. This analysis explores strategies and insights for parents who wish to transcend the legacy of emotionally immature and abusive parents and provide their children with a secure and emotionally fulfilling environment.

Self-awareness and Self-Healing: Self-awareness is the first step in breaking the cycle of abusive or emotionally immature parenting. Recognising how your upbringing has impacted your emotional well-being and parenting style is fundamental. Seek therapy or counselling to work through unresolved traumas and develop healthier coping mechanisms. Self-healing is essential, as it lays the foundation for providing a nurturing environment for your children.

Educate Yourself: To be an effective parent, educating yourself about healthy parenting practices is crucial. Read books, attend parenting workshops, and seek guidance from professionals specialising in child development and family dynamics. Understanding the principles of attachment theory, positive discipline, and emotional intelligence can be immensely beneficial.

Practice Emotional Regulation: Emotionally immature parents often struggle with regulating their own emotions, leading to erratic and sometimes abusive behaviour. Practice emotional regulation techniques such as mindfulness, deep breathing, and cognitive restructuring. Modelling emotional self-control for your children can help them develop these essential skills.

Break the Silence: Many abusive families maintain secrecy and silence about their problems. Break this cycle by openly discussing emotions and concerns with your children. Create an environment where your children feel safe expressing their feelings and fears without judgment, this fosters healthy communication and emotional development.

Set Healthy Boundaries: Emotionally immature parents may struggle with boundaries by being overly permissive or excessively authoritarian. Learning to set and enforce healthy limits for your children will be very beneficial; this involves balancing love and discipline, allowing children to explore their autonomy while providing guidance and structure.

Cultivate Empathy and Compassion: Developing empathy and compassion is crucial in parenting beyond the legacy of abuse. Put yourself in your child's shoes, acknowledge their feelings, and validate their experiences. Teach them the importance of empathy by modelling it in your interactions.

Seek Support Networks: Building a support network is vital for parents who are trying to break the cycle of abuse. Connect with other parents who share your journey, seek therapy or support groups, and lean on close friends and family members who can provide emotional support.

Prioritise Self-Care: Often, as parents, we put ourselves last, and it is vital to remember that taking care of ourselves is not selfish, and it is essential for effective parenting. Ensure you get enough rest, maintain a healthy lifestyle, and engage in activities that bring you joy and relaxation. A well-rested and emotionally balanced parent can provide better care for their children.

Continual Self-Reflection and Growth: Parenting is an ongoing process. Continually reflect on your actions and interactions with your children. Be open to feedback and adapt your parenting style as needed. Growth and change are part of the journey to breaking the cycle of emotionally immature or abusive parenting.

The parenting toolbox

It is crucial for anyone who has experienced abuse or had emotionally immature and toxic parents.

Here's why it's important:

Break the Cycle: If you've experienced abuse or toxicity in your upbringing, it's essential to break the cycle to prevent passing down harmful behaviours and patterns to your children. Developing a healthy parenting toolbox provides children with a more nurturing and supportive environment.

Ensure Your Child's Well-being: Children thrive in loving, safe, and nurturing environments. A healthy parenting toolbox equips you with the skills and strategies to create such an environment, which is vital for your child's emotional, psychological, and physical well-being.

Improve Your Well-being: Building a healthy parenting toolbox can also benefit your well-being. It allows you to heal from past trauma and develop healthier ways of relating to yourself and everyone around you, including your children. It's an opportunity for personal growth and healing.

Foster Healthy Relationships: Parenting is not just about raising children; it's also about building strong and healthy relationships with them. A healthy parenting toolbox helps cultivate a positive parent-child relationship based on trust, communication, and empathy.

Enhance Your Parenting Skills: Parenting is a skill that can be developed and improved over time. Investing in your parenting toolbox allows you to acquire practical communication skills, conflict resolution strategies, and other essential tools for successful parenting.

Provide Consistency and Stability: Children thrive on consistency and stability. A healthy parenting toolbox can help you establish routines, boundaries, and clear expectations, creating a secure and predictable environment for your child.

Address Your Triggers: Childhood trauma and abuse can lead to triggers that affect your parenting. Building a healthy parenting toolbox involves self-awareness and learning how to manage your triggers so you can respond to your child's needs in a balanced way.

Seek Support and Guidance: Building a healthy parenting toolbox may involve seeking support and guidance from professionals such as therapists, counsellors, or support groups.

These resources can provide valuable and very useful insights and strategies tailored to your specific circumstances.

Emotional intelligence: Fostering emotional intelligence in ourselves and our children is vital to our overall development and growth. Emotional intelligence, often called EQ (Emotional Quotient), encompasses the ability to understand, recognise, manage, and express emotions in healthy ways. It plays a significant role in the individual's social and emotional well-being, interpersonal relationships, and success in various life domains. As a parent, here's how you can achieve this and some psychological and emotional tools you could use:

Model Emotional Intelligence: Children learn by example. Demonstrate emotional intelligence in your own life by managing your emotions effectively, expressing empathy, and resolving conflicts constructively. Your behaviour serves as a powerful teaching tool.

Emotion Recognition: Teach children to recognise and label their emotions. Use picture books, storytelling, or discussions to help them identify different feelings in themselves and others.

Emotional Vocabulary: Expand their emotional vocabulary by introducing various emotion words. Encourage them to express how they feel using specific terms, such as "frustrated," "excited," or "sad."

Active Listening: Practice listening when your child wants to discuss their feelings. Give them your full attention, validate their emotions, and avoid judgment or criticism.

Encourage Expression: Create a safe and open environment where your child feels comfortable to express their emotions. Let them know that all feelings are valid and that handling a wide range of emotions is okay.

Problem-Solving Skills: Teach problem-solving skills to help children navigate challenging situations. Encourage them to brainstorm solutions and consider the consequences of their actions.

Empathy Development: Foster empathy by encouraging your child to consider how others might be feeling. Discussing the perspectives and emotions of fictional characters in books or movies could be a great way to do this.

Emotion Regulation: Help children develop strategies for regulating their emotions, such as deep breathing, mindfulness exercises, or taking a break when they feel overwhelmed.

Conflict Resolution: Teach conflict resolution skills, emphasising the importance of compromise, active listening, and finding mutually acceptable solutions.

Emotional Stories: Share stories or books that explore emotional themes. Discuss the characters' emotions, choices, and outcomes: this can provide valuable lessons in empathy and decision-making.

Emotion Coaching: Practice emotion coaching by acknowledging your child's feelings, validating them, and helping them find appropriate ways to manage them.

Encourage Emotional Expression in Art: Art, such as drawing, painting, or journaling, can provide a creative outlet for children to express their emotions when they find it difficult to verbalise them.

Reflective Conversations: Engage in thoughtful conversations with your child about their emotions and experiences. Help them explore the reasons behind their feelings and develop a deeper understanding of themselves.

Be Patient and Supportive: Remember that developing emotional intelligence is ongoing; be patient, offer support, and celebrate their progress.

Fostering emotional intelligence in children contributes to their psychological and emotional well-being. It equips them with essential life skills for building healthy relationships and navigating the world's complexities. It is a valuable gift that parents can provide to help their children thrive emotionally and socially.

In summary, building a healthy parenting toolbox is of paramount importance for all individuals who have experienced abuse or toxicity in their upbringing. It benefits your children and supports your own healing and personal growth. Remember that seeking professional guidance and support can be a crucial part of this process, as it can provide you with the tools and knowledge needed to be the best parent you can be.

Parenting beyond the legacy of emotionally immature and abusive parents is a challenging but worthwhile endeavour. It requires self-awareness, education, self-healing, and a commitment to create a nurturing and safe environment for your children. By implementing these insights and strategies, you can break the cycle and provide your children with the love, security, and emotional support they need to thrive. Remember that every parent makes mistakes, but the willingness to learn, grow, and prioritise your child's well-being can make all the difference.

CHAPTER 8

Embracing a Brighter Future

Celebrating progress and growth in the recovery journey from abuse is crucial for several significant reasons, and here's why it's important:

Validation of Efforts: Celebrating progress acknowledges the survivor's hard work and dedication to healing. It validates the effort we have put into our recovery, reinforcing that our journey matters and is worth recognising.

Boosts Self-Esteem: Survivors of abuse often struggle with low self-esteem and self-worth. Celebrating progress helps boost our self-esteem by highlighting our achievements, no matter how small. It allows us to see our value and capabilities more clearly.

Positive Reinforcement: Celebrating progress serves as positive reinforcement for healthy behaviours and coping strategies. Survivors are more likely to continue healing when our efforts lead to positive outcomes.

Motivation to Continue: Recognising and celebrating growth motivates us to keep moving forward. It reminds survivors of the positive changes they've experienced and encourages them to persevere through challenging times.

Fosters Resilience: Celebrating progress helps survivors build resilience. It shows them they can overcome adversity and reinforces their ability to adapt and thrive despite past trauma.

Reduces Self-Criticism: Many survivors of abuse are constantly battling with self-criticism and self-blame. Celebrating progress shifts the focus from self-blame to self-compassion, encouraging a kinder and more forgiving attitude toward oneself.

Enhances Self-Awareness: Recognising progress and growth encourages self-reflection. Survivors can better understand themselves, their strengths, and their resilience as they celebrate their journey.

Sense of Control: Celebrating progress empowers survivors by highlighting their agency and control over their lives. It emphasises that they can shape their recovery and future. Focusing on progress and growth promotes and cultivates a more positive outlook. It encourages survivors to envision a future where healing and happiness are achievable.

Reduces Feelings of Helplessness: Abuse can lead to feelings of helplessness and vulnerability. Celebrating progress counteracts these feelings by emphasising the survivor's ability to effect positive change.

Inspires Others: Sharing stories of progress and growth can inspire and provide hope to others on their recovery journey. It contributes to a sense of community and support among survivors.

In summary, celebrating progress and growth is an essential part of the healing process for survivors of abuse. It is a powerful tool for boosting self-esteem, motivation, and resilience while fostering self-compassion and a positive outlook on the future. It empowers survivors to take control of their recovery journey.

Building a life of happiness and fulfilment

Building a life of happiness and fulfilment after recovering from the abuse of emotionally immature, toxic, and abusive parents is both a challenging and rewarding journey. It involves reclaiming your sense of self, healing emotional wounds, and making choices that prioritise your well-being and happiness. It is a deeply personal and ongoing process. It's about reclaiming your power, making choices that align with your well-being, and finding joy in self-discovery and growth. Remember that you deserve happiness and that creating a life that reflects your true self and values is possible.

Establishing and maintaining healthy boundaries is fundamental in defining acceptable and unacceptable behaviour from others. Prioritising self-care practices that nurture your physical, emotional, and mental well-being is essential. Explore and process the healing of emotional wounds left by the abusive relationship; this may involve grieving, forgiveness (if you choose), and addressing any lingering trauma or self-esteem issues.

Reflect on your values, desires, and aspirations. What kind of life do you want to create for yourself? Knowing your values can guide your decisions and actions. Define short and long-term goals that align with your values; working toward these goals can provide a sense of purpose and direction. Build and nurture healthy, supportive relationships. Surround yourself with people who uplift and respect you. Seek joy and fulfilment and make time for activities and pursuits that bring you joy and fulfilment. Rediscover your passions and interests.

Work on challenging and reframing negative beliefs about yourself that your parents' abuse may have instilled in you. Recognise your worth and potential. Embrace your independence and autonomy. Take ownership of your life and the choices you make.

Continue using techniques helpful in your recovery journey, such as journaling, mindfulness, or self-reflection. Consider giving back to others in need or advocating for causes that are meaningful to you. Helping others can be a source of fulfilment and purpose. Acknowledge and celebrate your progress and achievements, however small they may seem. Each step forward is a testament to your efforts and, most importantly, stay patient; healing and rebuilding take time. Be patient with yourself and recognise that setbacks are a normal part of the journey.

Work continuously on self-improvement

Working on self-improvement continuously when recovering from abuse is of paramount importance. The recovery journey from abuse can be a long and challenging one, and self-improvement plays a vital role in the healing process.

Reclaiming Personal Power: Abuse can leave survivors feeling powerless and helpless. Self-improvement empowers individuals to regain control over their lives and choices. It allows them to be active participants in their recovery journey. Self-improvement activities can help rebuild a positive self-image and reinforce a sense of value and worthiness by restoring self-worth.

Healing Emotional Wounds: abuse leaves emotional scars that may require ongoing attention and healing. Self-improvement practices, such as therapy, self-reflection, and self-compassion, provide tools for addressing these emotional wounds. Survivors may have developed unhealthy coping mechanisms to deal with abuse. Self-improvement involves replacing these maladaptive coping strategies with healthier alternatives, such as mindfulness, self-regulation, and resilience-building.

Enhancing Resilience: Self-improvement fosters resilience, the ability to bounce back from adversity. Resilience is an invaluable asset in navigating the ups and downs of life and coping with future challenges effectively.

Embracing a Growth Mindset: A growth mindset involves the belief that development and personal growth are ongoing processes. It addresses individuals to view setbacks as opportunities for learning rather than failures.

Setting and Achieving Goals: Self-improvement often involves setting and working toward personal goals. Setting, pursuing, and achieving these goals can be a source of motivation, satisfaction, and purpose.

Fostering Independence: Self-improvement supports the development of independence and autonomy. Survivors can become self-reliant and less dependent on external validation or approval.

Creating a Positive Future: Continuous self-improvement is an investment in a positive future. It involves envisioning the kind of life one wants to lead and taking steps to make that vision a reality.

Empowering Self-Advocacy: Survivors of abuse may need to advocate for their own needs and rights. Self-improvement includes developing assertiveness and practical communication skills to express needs and boundaries.

Avoiding Re-Victimisation: Self-improvement helps individuals recognise and avoid situations or relationships that may traumatise them again. It involves learning to identify red flags and make choices that prioritise safety and well-being.

Strengthening Relationships: Individuals who work on self-improvement develop healthier relationship patterns. They become better at setting boundaries, communicating, and forming connections with others who respect and support their growth.

Enhancing Overall Well-Being: Ultimately, self-improvement contributes to overall well-being. It encompasses physical, emotional, and psychological health, fostering a holistic approach and a more fulfilling and satisfying life.

It's important to note that self-improvement is not a one-size-fits-all process. Each survivor's journey is unique, and the path to healing and self-growth may vary. Seeking support from therapists, counsellors, support groups, or trusted friends and family members can be valuable in this ongoing process.

Recovering from abuse is not just about surviving; it's about thriving and building a life that reflects one's true potential and worth. Continuous self-improvement is vital to achieve this transformation and create a future defined by strength, resilience, and happiness

Inspiring others to break their cycles

Inspiring others to break their cycles of abuse is a profound act of empathy and compassion and a transformative endeavour with far-reaching rewards, both for the individuals involved and future generations. Here are the tips and the importance of this inspiring journey:

Breaking the Cycle: The most immediate and significant reward is breaking the cycle of abuse. By inspiring others to confront and overcome their own experiences of abuse, you empower them to interrupt the harmful patterns that have plagued their lives and their families for generations.

Healing and Empowerment: Helping others on their journey to recovery and empowerment can be incredibly rewarding. Witnessing their growth and transformation can bring your life a deep sense of fulfilment and purpose.

Emotional Connection: Inspiring others to break the cycle of abuse fosters emotional connections and bonds rooted in shared experiences and resilience. These connections can be a source of support and understanding for both parties.

Ripple Effect: Breaking the cycle of abuse creates a ripple effect. When one person breaks free, they often inspire and support others in their family or community to do the same, leading to healing and transformation.

Legacy of Resilience: By inspiring others to break the cycle of abuse, you contribute to a legacy of resilience and strength. Your actions become a testament to the power of the human spirit to overcome adversity.

Empowering Future Generations: Breaking the cycle of abuse is crucial for the well-being of future generations. When individuals choose healing and growth over perpetuating abuse, they create a healthier environment for their children and grandchildren.

Modelling Healthy Relationships: Inspiring others to break the cycle of abuse involves modelling healthy relationship dynamics. Survivors who build and maintain healthy relationships provide a positive example for future generations.

Creating Safe Spaces: Breaking the cycle of abuse involves creating safe spaces for individuals to heal and share their experiences. These safe spaces can serve as foundations for support networks and communities dedicated to ending abuse.

Advocacy and Awareness: Those who break the cycle become advocates for abuse prevention and awareness. They can contribute to efforts to change societal attitudes, policies, and support systems related to abuse.

Personal Growth: Inspiring others to break the cycle of abuse can lead to personal growth and self-discovery. It can deepen your understanding of resilience, empathy, and the human capacity for transformation.

Fulfilling Purpose: Inspiring others to heal and grow is a life purpose for many survivors. It provides meaning and direction, allowing them to turn their past pain into a force for positive change.

Reducing Suffering: Ultimately, the most profound reward is the reduction of suffering. By inspiring others to break free from the shackles of abuse, you contribute to the alleviation of pain, trauma, and generational suffering.

In conclusion, inspiring others to break their cycles of abuse is an act of immense significance and compassion. It is a testament to the strength of the human spirit to transcend adversity and create a better future. By breaking the cycle and empowering future generations to do the same, we can shape a world where abuse can transform into resilience, healing, and hope.

Epilogue

In the concluding pages of "Healing the Past: The 6 Steps Healing Guide to Overcoming the Legacy of Emotionally Immature, Toxic, and Abusive Parents," the author extends heartfelt gratitude to readers for embarking on this deeply personal journey toward healing and reflects on the transformative journey embarked upon within the pages of this guide. It's a journey marked by profound introspection, courageous confrontation of painful memories, and the resilient pursuit of healing.

The epilogue reflects on the profound impact of the six transformative steps outlined within the book. It acknowledges the courage, vulnerability, and resilience displayed by individuals seeking to break free from the shadows of a challenging upbringing. It serves as a beacon of hope, and it celebrates their determination to break free from the chains of emotional immaturity, toxicity, and abuse passed down through generations.

This isn't just a guidebook; it's a testament to the human spirit's capacity for growth and healing. It honours the complexities of the past while illuminating a path toward understanding, forgiveness, and self-compassion. The epilogue emphasizes that healing isn't a linear process—it's a continuous evolution, an ongoing commitment to self-discovery and self-care. In these closing pages, the author emphasizes that healing is about understanding and acknowledging the past and reclaiming agency over one's present and future. It's about discovering the power within to rewrite one's story, foster healthy relationships, and embrace a life filled with joy, authenticity, and purpose.

Through the author's compassionate voice, the epilogue invites readers to recognize their progress, regardless of the stage of their healing journey. It encourages them to celebrate every step forward, every moment of clarity, and every instance of self-empowerment. The epilogue encapsulates the essence of the healing journey, reminding readers that while scars may linger, they no longer define or confine. It inspires a vision of a life unshackled from the shadows of the past, where happiness, self-love, and the ability to live fully reign supreme.

Above all, the epilogue serves as a reminder that while the scars of the past may linger, they do not define one's future. It offers hope that by embracing the wisdom gained from the journey, individuals can pave a new path filled with self-love, authenticity, and the freedom to live on their terms. Ultimately, the epilogue is a testament to the resilience of the human spirit, offering solace and encouragement to all who have traversed the pages, urging them to continue their journey towards understanding, healing, and the unwavering pursuit of a fulfilling and abundant life.

Closing with words of encouragement and empowerment, the epilogue instils a sense of possibility, urging readers to carry the lessons learned into their futures—a future marked by healing, happiness, and the profound ability to live life fully, liberated from the confines of an emotionally tumultuous past.

To Leo

Never underestimate a cycle breaker. Not only did they experience years of generational trauma, but they stood in the face of trauma and fought to say "This ends with me.

Fun fact:

Did you know that providing something valuable to another person makes you more valuable to them?

By leaving your honest opinion of this book on Amazon, you'll show other victims where they can find the tools and information, they need to become empowered, healed survivors and live more full-felt, meaningful lives.

So if you belive this book could help another victime/ survivour of abuse send it their way. It's time to pass on your newfound knowledge and show other readers where they can find the same help.

Scan the QR code bellow to leave your review.

Thank you from the bottom of my heart.

Norma Caceres-Pell

Resources and further Support

Resources and recommended Books to Help You Understand Toxic Relationships Aren't Your Fault and Give You the Coping and Grieving Tools to Move Forward

Living Better Lives NWA. (2021, April 6). The 4 Types of Emotionally Immature Parents. *Living Better Lives NWA*. Retrieved from

https://www.livingbetterlivesnwa.com/blog/2021/4/6/the-4-types-of-emotionally-immature-parents

Shortform. (n.d.). Four Types of Emotionally Immature Parents. *Shortform Blog*. Retrieved from

https://www.shortform.com/blog/four-types-of-emotionally-immature-parents/

Parenting For Brain. (n.d.). Emotionally Immature Parents. *Parenting For Brain*. Retrieved from

https://www.parentingforbrain.com/emotionally-immature-parents/

Overcoming Toxic People. (n.d.). Signs of a Narcissist - 21 Behaviors of the Classical Narcissist. *Overcoming Toxic People*. Retrieved from

https://overcomingtoxicpeople.com/Narcissists/Signs_of_a_Narcis
sist___21_Behaviors_of_the_Classical_Narcissist.html

Healthline. (n.d.). Covert Narcissist. *Healthline*. Retrieved from

https://www.healthline.com/health/covert-narcissist#covert-
narcissism

Healthline. (n.d.). Malignant Narcissism. *Healthline*. Retrieved
from

https://www.healthline.com/health/malignant-narcissism#traits

TEDx Talks. (2016, March 17). The Narcissism Epidemic: Living
in the Age of Entitlement | Mitzi B. [Video]. YouTube.

 https://www.youtube.com/watch?v=IEfS-_a21kk

TEDx Talks. (2014, June 19). Emotional Intelligence: Using the
Laws of Attraction | D. Ivan Young | TEDxLSCTomball [Video].
YouTube.

 https://www.youtube.com/watch?v=2R1tjOH4wT8

Healthline. (n.d.). Sociopath. *Healthline*. Retrieved from
https://www.healthline.com/health/mental-health/sociopath

Dr. Axe. (n.d.). What Is a Sociopath? *Dr. Axe*. Retrieved from
https://draxe.com/health/what-is-a-sociopath/

Verywell Mind. (n.d.). What Are the Effects of Childhood
Trauma? *Verywell Mind*. Retrieved from

https://www.verywellmind.com/what-are-the-effects-of-childhood-trauma-4147640

Goalcast. (n.d.). Psychological Trauma: How It Affects Your Mind and Body. *Goalcast*. Retrieved from

 https://www.goalcast.com/psychological-trauma/

The Virago. (n.d.). The Root of a Narcissist's Behavior. *Medium*. Retrieved from https://medium.com/the-virago/the-root-of-a-narcissists-behavior-adefa4eee842

Psych Central. (2019, November). How Emotionally Immature Parents Raise Emotionally Neglected Kids. *Psych Central Blog*. Retrieved from

https://psychcentral.com/blog/childhood-neglect/2019/11/how-emotionally-immature-parents-raise-emotionally-neglected-kids#1

Psychology Today. (n.d.). Child Neglect. *Psychology Today*. Retrieved from

https://www.psychologytoday.com/us/conditions/child-neglect

Healthline. (n.d.). Childhood Emotional Neglect. *Healthline*. Retrieved from

 https://www.healthline.com/health/mental-health/childhood-emotional-neglect

Psych Central. (2020, April). How to Set Boundaries With Toxic People. *Imperfect*. Retrieved from

https://psychcentral.com/blog/imperfect/2020/04/how-to-set-boundaries-with-toxic-people#W

A Point of Light. (n.d.). How to Set Boundaries With Toxic People. *A Point of Light*. Retrieved from
https://apointoflight.co/set-boundaries-toxic-people/

Azevedo Family Psychology. (n.d.). 3 Tips for Setting Boundaries With Toxic Family Members. *Azevedo Family Psychology*. Retrieved from

https://www.azevedofamilypsychology.com/family-psychology/3-tips-for-setting-boundaries-with-toxic-family-members

Focus on Integrative Healthcare. (n.d.). Trauma and Autoimmune Diseases. *Focus on Integrative Healthcare*. Retrieved from

https://www.focusih.com/trauma-autoimmune/#:~:text=Up%20to%2080%25%20of%20adults%20in%20one%20study,then%20leads%20to%20autoimmune%20destruction%20of%20body%20tissues.

Well.Org. (n.d.). Stress, Trauma, & Autoimmune Conditions. *Well.Org*. Retrieved from

 https://well.org/medicine/stress-trauma-autoimmune-conditions/

National Institute of Environmental Health Sciences (NIEHS). (n.d.). Autoimmune Diseases. *National Institute of Environmental Health Sciences (NIEHS)*. Retrieved from

https://www.niehs.nih.gov/health/topics/conditions/autoimmune/index.cfm

Psychology Today. (2018, November). Forgiveness: The Path to Healing and Emotional Freedom. *Psychology Today*. Retrieved from

https://www.psychologytoday.com/us/blog/surviving-thriving/201811/forgiveness-the-path-healing-and-emotional-freedom

Psychology Today. (2020, December). 5 Reasons Why It's Important to Let Go of the Past. *Psychology Today*. Retrieved from

https://www.psychologytoday.com/us/blog/in-flux/202012/5-reasons-why-its-important-let-go-the-past

Psychology Today. (2020, December). 5 Reasons Why It's Important to Let Go of the Past. *Psychology Today*. Retrieved from

https://www.psychologytoday.com/us/blog/in-flux/202012/5-reasons-why-its-important-let-go-the-past

Verywell Mind. (n.d.). How Forgiveness Impacts Mental Health and Relieves Stress. *Verywell Mind*. Retrieved from https://www.verywellmind.com/how-forgiveness-impacts-mental-health-and-relieves-stress-7497219

Moodcafe. (n.d.). Safe Space Imagery. *Moodcafe*. Retrieved from https://www.moodcafe.co.uk/media/50868/4.3%20Safe%20Space%20Imagery.pdf

McBride, K. (2009). *Will I Ever Be Good Enough?: Healing the Daughters of Narcissistic Mothers*. HCI; Reprint edition.

Gibson, L. C. (2015). *Adult Children of Emotionally Immature Parents: How to Heal from Distant, Rejecting, or Self-Involved Parents*. New Harbinger Publications.

Campbell, S. (2019). *But It's Your Family…: Cutting Ties with Toxic Family Members and Loving Yourself in the Aftermath*. Mango.

Forward, S., & Buck, C. (2002). *Toxic Parents: Overcoming Their Hurtful Legacy and Reclaiming Your Life*. Bantam.

Webb, J. (2012). *Running on Empty: Overcome Your Childhood Emotional Neglect*. Morgan James Publishing.

Winfrey, O., & Perry, B. D. (Year of Publication). *What Happened to You?: Conversations on Trauma, Resilience, and Healing*. Flatiron Books.

Hunt, B. J. (2017). *Forgiveness Made Easy: The Revolutionary Guide to Moving Beyond Your Past and Truly Letting Go.* Publisher Name.

Webb, J. (2017). *Running on Empty No More: Transform Your Relationships With Your Partner, Your Parents, and Your Children.* Morgan James Publishing.

van der Kolk, B. (2015). *The Body Keeps the Score: Brain, Mind, and Body in the Healing of Trauma.* Penguin Books.

Rice, O. K., & Cardia, J. L. 2021. *Absent: How to Heal from Emotionally Toxic Parents: A Grown-Up's Guide to Healing from Childhood Neglect, Manipulation, Trauma and Abusive Emotional Behavior.* Publisher Name.

Printed in Great Britain
by Amazon

40070528R00108